THE PATH OF ASCENT

The Five Principles
for Mastering Change

THE PATH OF ASCENT
The Five Principles for Mastering Change

"This book is a great resource for managers leading change."

Richard Parkinson
President and CEO, Associated Food Stores

"The heart of leadership is the capacity to influence change. If you want to be a better leader, your investment in this book is one of the best returns you'll ever get."

Joseph Grenny
New York Times bestselling co-author of *Influencer: The Power to Change Anything*

"Juan Riboldi has given us the fruit of his career in studying and working with leaders and industries. Just given his track record and exposure would be enough to say read this book. Looking at not only what makes a successful leader, but what environment/culture allows that successful leader to succeed or commits them to failure is extremely valuable and there is much to learn from it."

Sr. Carol Keehan, D.C.
President/CEO, The Catholic Health Association of the United States

"Juan Riboldi clearly shows his expertise in culture change. This book delivers great insight into what makes change stick in a company culture. The analysis is a must for performance-oriented leadership."

Robin Johnson
Chief Executive Officer, Financial Times Search / Newssift

"*The Path of Ascent* is a must read for leaders wanting to visualize and realize successful change. Through examples trending both winning organizations as well as declining organizations, *The Path of Ascent* identifies the five principles needed for mastering change and achieving desired outcomes."

Sharon Gardner
Vice President, Human Resources, Yuma Regional Medical Center

"Juan combines his deep personal insights and expertise of successful leadership and organizational change behaviors with grounded theory and real-world application. An important read especially in these turbulent and demanding times."

Mike Rude

Vice President, Human Resources, Stryker Corporation

"This is powerful advice for any organization embarking on a major change initiative."

Jeanne Scott

Vice President, Human Resources, El Pollo Loco

"Mr. Riboldi's Five Ascent Principles work as an extremely effective means to deal with organizational change. The principles were very well-received, particularly by senior executives. I would definitely recommend this process to any executive who needs to apply structure to the most uncertain of times."

Patrick Gallagher

Vice President, Human Resources, Financial Times

"*The Path of Ascent* is clear and balanced, highly readable, and just makes sense. Successful change is simply a choice!"

Teri Norris, MSA, SPHR

Director of Talent Management, Yuma Regional Medical Center

"This book delivers practical insights and well researched answers that will benefit any organization going through change."

Robyn Warr

Human Resources Director, PHR® Lenox Advisors

"This book takes a comprehensive look at the nature of change and how we can positively respond to it. I highly recommended it for anyone desiring change mastery!"

Marilyn Holland

Quality Assurance Specialist, 1st Global

"Juan has real-world experience in bringing change to organizations. He delivered a 360-multi-rater assessment program to our managers so that we could drive change in our agency based on candid feedback from our line employees. I highly recommend Juan's take on leading organizational change."

Tom Zrubek

Leadership Coach

"Juan's principles are based on real-life experience of the successes and failures of 50 companies which underwent radical change. This book is an easy and essential read for any leader faced with major organizational change. It provides a simple roadmap to success."

Denise Phelps
Director, Center for Organizational Development,
Mercy Medical Center

"This book provides a clear and practical approach for implementing organizational change in today's fast-paced and unpredictable business world."

Kevin Ricklefs
Vice President, Administration, CHG Healthcare Services

"When organizations are viewed as living systems, not just financial entities, people can become more present of their own part in growing and evolving them. Over the years of working with Juan, I have so appreciated his ability to truly listen to people, to be sensitive to the changes within organizational ecosystems, and to support positive natural growth. This book is an excellent resource for anyone leading a culture through change."

Tom James
Former COO of Crown Packaging and author of *Quick! Fix the Hippo: Leadership Instincts and Organizational Ecosystems*

THE PATH OF ASCENT

The Five Principles for Mastering Change

*How People and Organizations Prosper
. . . and Why Most Don't*

Juan Riboldi

For additional information contact:
Ascent Advisor
800-679-2881
info@ascent-advisor.com
1482 East 950 South
Provo, UT 84606

Library of Congress Catalog-in-Publication Data
Riboldi, Juan, 2009
The Path of Ascent: The Five Principles for Mastering Change
3rd ed.
p.cm.

1. Organizational change. 2. Leadership. 3. Management

TX 7-122-525
ISBN 978-0-9824647-0-0

*I dedicate this work to the three women
who changed my life for the better.
To my grandmother Elsa,
to my mother, Liliana,
and to my wife, Sherilyn.
In a broader sense,
I dedicate this work to every
reader seeking useful ideas
for improving how we work and live.*

Contents

Introduction

How can you tell if a change is going to succeed or fail?

If you know what to look for, you can recognize the path you are currently taking. Then you will be able to realize your present destination and if necessary, steer in the right direction. This single, most valuable insight can save you and your organization unnecessary frustration and painful losses.

This book reveals the keys for making change work in today's fast-changing environment. Based on his wide experience consulting with leaders of organizations large and small, and his research into 50 organizations that undertook major transformations, Juan Riboldi presents a step-by-step course for long-lasting and positive change.

In *The Path of Ascent,* we learn how the best leaders and organizations prospered from change and why most don't. Organizations and individuals must look to those who have been successful to learn the proven principles for mastering change.

The most successful teams and organizations have followed a distinctive pattern for change—a steady upward climb toward loftier goals. In other words, they took *The Path of Ascent.* This course describes the Five Ascent Principles™, which, when applied correctly, will help a leader, a team, or an organization make the most of the opportunity for change.

The Path of Ascent provides the framework for teams and organizations to begin their own upward climb to greater success. Above all, The Path of Ascent teaches individuals and organizations how to change for the better and overcome the challenges, pressures, and difficulties of the modern global marketplace.

Acknowledgments

Bringing about this book is the result of the combined contributions of many friends and colleagues. It is with gratitude that I give credit to all those who provided their time and resources generously. Their assistance has made this work possible and enriched me personally.

First of all, I express heartfelt thanks to Sherilyn, my loving companion of over 20 years, whose support throughout our marriage has been kind, valuable, and constant. Particularly during the extensive period devoted to writing this book, she has been a caring partner, encouraging friend, and wise advisor. I am fortunate to have married her. To my children, too, goes my gratitude, as they have unknowingly encouraged me, through their excitement, to do my very best on this endeavor.

In addition, I thank professional colleagues who have provided, over the years, powerful formative experiences and insights. Among the more notable colleagues, I acknowledge Kerry Patterson, Joseph Grenny, Ron McMillan, and Al Switzler, the four founding partners of VitalSmarts, through whom I learned critical skills that helped me become a better person and a more influential consultant. I thank Tom James for the opportunity of working closely with him for over three years, facilitating a successful turnaround at Crown Packaging. Tom and I have carried on many energizing conversations, late into the evening, about the change process. I recognize Karen Donaldson, whose insightful coaching has helped me clarify existing ideas and discover additional ones. I thank Tracy Maylett, my partner at DecisionWise, for his reliable support as I devoted myself to research and writing.

I give my sincere appreciation to leaders at several client organizations. They opened the doors of opportunity for me to apply the principles and practices that shaped my learning. I appreciate their willingness to be interviewed and share their best practices openly. Through a variety of client experiences I have been able to collect the raw materials that made this book possible.

The actual writing of this book has been a process of continuous improvements, going through multiple discussions, revisions, and iterations. In this regard, I make special mention of Katie Chandler, whose work as a literary coach provided pointed comments and editorial feedback on a weekly basis for an entire year. Through her thoughtful input and keen eye for detail, my writing improved significantly as key concepts came into sharper focus. In addition, I thank the generous contribution of a group of reviewers including Craig Perkes, Tanille Rodman, and Pablo Riboldi for their insightful feedback.

For the fine editing and typesetting of this work, I want to acknowledge the talent of Jacob Rawlins and Laura Rawlins, whose expertise as book editors refined the language, improved the flow and designed the pages. Through numerous editing rounds they turned a rough manuscript into a quality reading material. For the impactful design of the book identity, I give credit to Keoki Williams, whose superb ability to convey a concept in a graphic is unmatched.

At the time of completing this first edition, I recognize that the labor of publishing, distributing, and promoting this book will involve many others. I express in advance my gratitude for the valuable support of all in taking this book forward.

## PART ONE

A Change for the Better

## CHAPTER ONE

Choosing to Ascend

*To change and to improve
are two different things.*

~German proverb

Recognizing the Pattern of Change

All change is not progress. Can you tell the difference between the two?

Much of what is changing in today's world is not for the better. To ascend, change must result in a sustainable improvement. This book reveals the essential differences between the people and organizations that ascend and those that merely change.

If you knew what to look for you could recognize the course you and your organization are on, and then steer in the right direction. The key is to know what to look for. The key is being able to recognize the pattern of change.

At work and in our lives, we are required to change. One way or another, we all have to change. The question is: will it be for better or worse? The answer hinges on a crucial choice we all make every day of our lives.

Have you ever considered why some people who are faced with unprecedented challenges grow and prosper while most struggle just to survive and many even fail? In a changing world, survival is a matter of constant adaptation. But merely coping with change does not lead to success. Everyone changes, but only a few governments, enterprises, teams, and individuals rise, even from the depth of adversity, to a higher level. The vast majority of change initiatives end up in disappointment. Understanding what makes the difference between the groups that fail and those that succeed has far-reaching implications for all of us.

Dave House is just one of those people who seemed destined to go from one success to another at work. His professional career was on the up and up. Then, something changed.

During 22 years at Intel, Dave House led the development of the world's leading microprocessor line, culminating with the Pentium processor, and managed the launch of one of the most successful advertising campaigns in the history of high technology—"Intel Inside." With such a track record, Dave was on the short list of Intel executive talent, but Intel CEO Andy Grove had made it plain that House would not succeed him. "It was time for Dave to go out and lead," said House's longtime friend Marty Ruberry.[1]

House left a supercharged Intel to become chairman, CEO, and president of then fledgling Bay Networks, a deeply troubled computer networking company desperately in need of a strong leader. Because Bay had missed product launches and had been experiencing quality problems, the company was quickly becoming prey to local rival and industry leader, Cisco Systems. Adding to Bay's troubles, employees were defecting in droves, customers were quickly losing faith, and, as House himself noted, leadership "spiraled down" to "almost chaos and anarchy."

Once he took the helm, House immediately began digging at the roots of Bay's troubles. He admitted that at first he did not know where to start. He asked for 60 days to talk with the customers and the employees to understand what was needed. Likewise, House sent out teams of executives to meet with customers and employees. After 60 days they had plenty of ideas of what needed fixing most. House and his team launched multiple rapid improvement initiatives.

House spotted internal fights between competing groups, which he ended immediately by prioritizing projects and getting everyone focused on the same goals. He required strict account-ability, asking his managers to set measurable goals for each quarter and for the year. As leaders worked with their respective staff to achieve specific objectives, House imposed strict Intel-like management discipline on his managers and taught his own management classes to the top 120 Bay executives.

Notice that House's initial actions rapidly improved employee focus on customer priorities, increased collaboration, and the discipline of accountability. All this happened without making large capital investments or launching heady strategic initiatives. Later on, House boosted Bay's product line through a series of savvy acquisitions and introduced an attractive employee stock options program as an incentive to stay with the company.

Within 15 months, the changes House initiated were bearing fruit: Bay earnings rose to $89 million, up from a $167 million loss the previous year; turnover dropped by about half to near the industry average; and customers became engaged once again as a result of Bay executive sales visits and an exciting new product line. Bay became an exciting place to work.

After turning Bay Networks around, House negotiated the merger of Bay and Nortel Networks, a merger that created a global Internet and communications industry leader with $8 billion in shareholder value. That made House president of an $18 billion company with operations in 150 countries.[2]

The newly formed company was highly profitable and innovative, transforming itself from a technology-focused company to an opportunity- and customer-focused enterprise. A March 21, 2000, Nortel Networks news release stated, "Nortel Networks is ranked number one globally in Optical Internet solutions, with more than 75% of North American Internet backbone traffic traveling across Nortel systems." The change was the result of an ambitious redesign of the company's entire product development process in order to significantly reduce time to market.

Pause! Freeze the story at this point and we must conclude that Dave House is a phenomenal turnaround leader, and Nortel Networks is set up for a huge success. In fact, as the year 2000 came to an end, Nortel was widely heralded as a financial super-star. With the global Internet market poised to expand at a 28% compound annual growth rate at that time, we could safely bet on Nortel Networks. Besides, the company kept reporting record gains and projecting strong results for the near future.

But while analysts were confidently predicting Nortel's con-tinued success, employees working inside the company were becoming increasingly concerned. Difficulties arising from Bay's and Nortel's vastly different cultures challenged every attempt at integration. Even before the acquisition, House and Nortel executives acknowledged the need to create a shared vision. Despite launching integration teams and a cultural alignment effort, change at Nortel was piecemeal and slow as opposed to the fast and comprehensive transformation at Bay. The antici-pated synergies of merging the two companies never material-ized and instead drained resources and diffused focus.

Additional clouds were gathering on the horizon. The rapid expansion at Nortel created excess production capacity at a time when the market suddenly turned cold. Signs of trouble spread into the boardroom. Amid differences of opinions, House quietly left the company. The board downplayed the potential impact of House' departure; they were more concerned with managing the business than leading a transformation.

The gathering clouds quickly turned into a raging storm. In 2001 Nortel spiraled into a downturn, laying off more than 10,000 workers. Over the following two years, Nortel stock lost 86% of its value, going from over $800 per share at its peak to less than $1. After a prolonged decline, Nortel finally filed for bankruptcy.

What went wrong at Nortel Networks? Starting off with so much momentum and while still looking at a promising future, Nortel's fortune suddenly turned into a devastating loss. The transformation expected to generate billions of dollars of share-holder value evaporated. Their advanced technology poised to capture the expanding Internet market faltered. More impor-tantly perhaps was the cost to thousands of people's hopes, dreams, and promises. Nortel's inability to make change work is at the core of the tragic story.

If this is a blessing,
it is certainly very well disguised.

~Winston Churchill

What is most striking about this story is the wholly unexpected twist of fortune. Dave House had demonstrated an innate talent to lead complex transformations to achieve amazing results. He had been doing it for over two decades! At Intel and at Bay Networks, House had faced much riskier challenges. At Nortel Networks, he was seemingly in the right place at the right time. So, what happened?

House certainly had clout and an impressive track record, but he encountered subtle obstacles at Nortel Networks that compromised his previously successful strategy for change. House believed that unless the acquisition delivered results from the start, Nortel's long-term strategy would not work. Nortel executives thought otherwise. House, then second in command, relented because he thought that they must know what they are doing. As he said, "A lot of other issues when you dig down deep enough have turf as their root cause."[3]

The success House experienced leading change at Intel and at Bay Networks had a lot to do with the people; more specifically, with their operating principles for change. Such principles were clearly missing at Nortel and became the cause of its downfall. House's departure signaled more than a career transition over a difference of opinion. It marked an entirely different approach to change.

Mastering Change

Change presents the ultimate human challenge. Since change is the primary process of life, mastering change is akin to mastering life. Studies of organizational change report that only one third of all change initiatives are truly successful; a full two thirds fail to deliver their expected results. Why is that?

When I first heard these statistics I was a college student studying organizational change. At the time, I thought that such a poor success rate indicated the inherent difficulty of making change work. Changing deeply entrenched personal habits is tough enough; changing the culture of an entire organization is exponentially more difficult. Consequently, my assumption at that time was that only the best and most tenacious succeed at making change work. Hard work and diligence was all it required, or so I thought.

Later on, while working as a management consultant, I learned that while change requires hard work, hard work alone does not necessarily lead to successful change. My clients and I worked diligently for years to improve organizations. We applied the best methodologies, used the best tools, and practiced the most advanced skills for transforming enterprises. In every case we committed a full measure of effort to the cause. But no matter how hard we worked, some changes succeeded and others did not. Something was missing.

After 20 years working in the trenches of corporate change projects, I set out to discover the answer. After a lengthy search, distilling the best thinking and practices in the field, and comparing their findings with my own experiences, I began to notice a pattern common to all successful changes. Likewise, failed initiatives showed distinctive characteristics.

Applying the correct process increased the likelihood of a successful change project. That was very encouraging. But soon I discovered that following a process step by step was not enough. The methodology alone was insufficient to guarantee success every time. Under similar conditions and following the same process, one project achieved great results and the next one didn't. Something beyond a mechanical process for change was required.

Looking through my research notes and personal experiences, I noticed that successful change hinges on people's choices. Regardless of investments in systems, tools, and processes, the rate of successful change has remained constant—at about one third. The mystery of successful change remained locked inside the human element.

When I began writing this book, I decided to settle the change question for good. I approached the subject with full confidence, but once I began writing, the work I had expected to complete in a few weeks expanded into several months and then spilled into well over a year. The nagging question continued whispering in my mind: "What makes change work?" I decided to go all out into a formal research project.

Good research starts with a hypothesis—an assumption of how things work. Then, data either confirm or contradict the initial assumption. Such has been the process leading to discovering the Path of Ascent.

In this case, the original premise behind this book came to me as a spark of insight after contemplating the subject for a long time. Ideas that I had been mulling over for years suddenly became clear as a set of five principles. These principles came to my mind so unexpectedly that I scribbled them down on a piece of paper I had nearby. With surprising ease, I quickly filled both sides of the single page with a precise description of each of the five principles and how they relate to each other. A few minutes later, I was done writing. I sat motionless pondering what I had just received, trying to grasp its full meaning. The chart below summarizes the Five Ascent Principles with their respective process step and outcome.

The Five Ascent Principles		
Process	Principle	Outcome
1. Envision	Creating the story of success	**Purpose**
2. Evaluate	Seizing the opportunity for change	**Direction**
3. Empower	Developing capacity from strengths	**Ability**
4. Engage	Inspiring teamwork and commitment	**Motivation**
5. Evolve	Achieving increasingly better results	**Results**

For more information on the research behind the Five Ascent Principles, see the appendix.

Instinctively, I knew that these five principles provided the answer to a longstanding question of mine. The stroke of insight was soon over, and I was left with the arduous challenge of conveying this new understanding. Thus, the writing of this book began.

With the Five Ascent Principles in mind, I began reviewing books and articles on the subject, questioning my own assumptions, and studying companies that changed successfully and those that didn't. This work resulted in over 700 pages of financial data, news clippings, and live interviews. I spent many late nights at the university library gaining greater understanding of the principles through the weight of factual evidence.

Through the course of this study, I identified 50 publicly traded companies that had embarked on significant change initiatives within the last 15 years. All the companies selected went through a period of radical transformation. I discarded from the pool companies that experienced only incremental improvements that merely reflected industry or general market trends.

The list included well-known, publicly traded companies for which there is ample financial data available. I discarded companies posting limited financial information or with insufficient news coverage. I needed to base the study on companies I could fully understand from multiple perspectives.

Finally, I defined each company's transformation period, which usually started with a trigger event—a change in leadership or strategy or, as is most often the case, an impending crisis. The period of intense, radical transformation for these companies usually lasted about three to four years. I decided to extend the study to a standard five-year period, or sixty months, to observe the near-term results of the transformation.

To define the degree of success of each transformation, I looked primarily at the company's financial performance as reflected by their stock price appreciation. Then, as a secondary measure, I took into account the company's overall performance by looking at a variety of financial and non-financial measures.

In deciding what I would consider real success, I assessed long-term sustainability as well. I refined the rankings by considering a company's performance for an additional 5 years after the initial 5-year transformation period. Market conditions aside, the change initiative had to be deemed an improvement for a total of 10 years from the starting point. Through this process, I upgraded a few companies' change rankings because the achievement stood the 10-year test. Likewise, I downgraded several notable companies whose gains were soon reversed because the changes were either insufficient, or because they were artificially rigged.

After weighing in all these considerations and finding the true gems, I decided to show the final ranking simply by displaying the company's stock price appreciation during the respective change period. I ranked the 50 transforming organizations by degree of success. Then, I compared the top 10 with the bottom 10 companies.

The object of my research was to compare the companies that succeeded with those that failed in order to identify what made the difference. All 50 companies publicly acknowledged that they were undertaking a vast transformation. They faced a similar economic environment. All 50 companies started off fully expecting dramatic improvement. But after a few years, only a third of these initiatives were truly successful. Many produced unimpressive results and a full third flatly failed.

The chart on the following page shows my research results for the 10 most successful organizational changes. The list represents definitive success during a time of radical organizational change. For each company selected, the chart shows the respective stock symbol, change period, and stock price appreciation. I refer to this select group of companies as the Change Masters.

On average, the Change Masters more than tripled the company's stock value during the change period. These companies outperformed the market significantly. In the case of Intel, their stock appreciation was almost tenfold!

In contrast to the Change Masters, the 10 biggest change failures show what happens when change does not work. During the specified time period, the change initiatives at these organizations produced very unsuccessful results. The stock

Change Masters

10 Most Successful Changes

#	Company	Symbol	Period	Stock Appreciation
1	Intel	INTC	1994–1999	921%
2	Apple	AAPL	2001–2005	565%
3	General Electric	GE	1995–1999	561%
4	IBM	IBM	1995–1999	528%
5	Caterpillar	CAT	2003–2007	264%
6	McDonald's	MCD	2003–2006	237%
7	VeriSign	VRSN	2003–2006	200%
8	Nissan	NSANY	2000–2004	190%
9	3M	MMM	2000–2004	88%
10	Xerox	XRX	2001–2005	81%
Average Gain from a Successful Change				**363%**

Change Failures

10 Biggest Change Failures

#	Company	Symbol	Period	Stock Depreciation
1	Nortel Networks	NT	1998–2002	-86%
2	3 Com	COMS	2001–2005	-67%
3	Dell	DELL	1999–2001	-45%
4	Ford	F	1999–2003	-43%
5	Eastman Kodak	EK	2000–2004	-41%
6	New York Times	NYT	2002–2006	-37%
7	General Motors	GM	2000–2004	-32%
8	RadioShack	RSH	2000–2004	-31%
9	Qwest Comm.	Q	2002–2006	-20%
10	Hewlett-Packard	HPQ	1999–2003	-20%
Average Loss from a Failed Change				**-42%**

depreciation resulted in severe losses, especially in the case of Nortel Networks, which showed a drastic 86% depreciation of stock price during the change period. Every company decline is significant, accounting for an average loss of 42% in stock price as a result of unsuccessful change. I refer to this group of companies as the Change Failures.

Comparing the two groups of companies, we can immediately discern the financial impact of changing successfully or not. As we add the average gain of the Change Masters to the average loss of the Change Failures, we come up with the total change gap—a 400% difference. Comparing Intel, the most successful change among the companies studied, with Nortel Networks, representing the biggest loss, we account for a 1,000% difference!

Contemplating the vast disparity between these two groups, one wonders if such results could have been predicted beforehand, and if so, what indicators might foretell the likelihood of success or the imminent risk of failure.

Riding the Roller Coaster

Ironically, the same person, Dave House, played a key role at both Intel and Nortel Networks, represented in the study as the most and the least successful changes. A deeper examination of what was happening inside and around Dave House at the time reveals important cues. Reading these subtle cues is crucial to recognizing the course we are on.

If you had been an employee working at Intel in 1994, you would have known that your company was making a dramatic shift from manufacturing memory chips to producing microprocessors. Several competitors had jumped on the promising opportunity, while others were going to compete fiercely in the commodity-priced memory market. Imagine you were at an Intel management retreat listening to the company executives unveil the new strategy and announce the required changes. Everyone realized the company was making a bold and risky decision. Would you have been able to predict then that your company would eventually dominate the microprocessor market to the point of devastating the competition?

Now, switch gears and picture yourself as a Nortel Networks employee in 1998. Your company had just announced the acquisition of Bay, a Silicon Valley darling. Management was expanding operations while launching several improvement initiatives. Analysts were buzzing with predictions of continued success. Watching all that was going on around you, would you have been able to predict that massive layoffs were just around the corner?

The point is, if you know what to look for, you can recognize the course your organization is on. You can forecast predictable consequences. If you don't like the projected results, you can change course. In order to anticipate the success of Intel or the failure of Nortel Networks, you need only to see the pattern of change.

Seeing the pattern of change requires an objective view of the overall trend. We need to step back from the moment and notice cause-and-effect relationships weaving seemingly insignificant actions into a solid pattern of conduct. The emerging picture describes the likely course of events.

Apply this concept to your organization, your team, or your own family. Step back from the moment—from what is happening right now—and see what is happening over time. What are the established patterns of conduct and where are they leading? If you can see the pattern of change, you can predict the likely outcomes.

To get a quick grasp of the change patterns, one needs only to look at the Change Patterns chart. At a glance, we can see the story of success or failure represented by the aggregate stock price trend of the Change Masters versus the Change Failures. We also see a dramatic reversal of fortune as failed change starts at a higher point and rises quickly, only to experience high volatility at the top and a sudden drop well below the steady and solid rise of the Change Masters.

The Change Patterns chart shows the 60-month stock price trend of the Change Masters and the Change Failures as if the companies were going through the change simultaneously. What becomes clear is a visual representation of two distinct paths— the Path of Ascent and the Roller Coaster Ride.

The chart shows how each group of companies approached change in a different way from the beginning. It wasn't that the

Change Patterns

Stock Price of Companies during Change Period

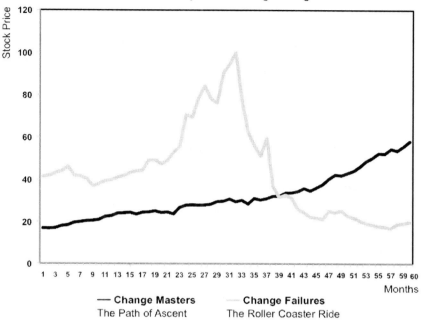

─── **Change Masters**   ⋯ **Change Failures**
The Path of Ascent   The Roller Coaster Ride

Change Masters were doing the same thing as the Change Failures, only faster or better. Instead, the Change Masters followed an essentially different pattern to changing.

This chart tells us that it is possible to visualize successful change—the Path of Ascent! And more importantly, it is possible to predict the success or failure of a change from the beginning, as long as we can identify the pattern of change the organization is pursuing.

The organizations that changed successfully show a gradual rise with minor bumps along the way. Progress is steady, making sustained improvement a predictable destination from the start. The Path of Ascent helps us visualize what successful, lasting change actually looks like. The Roller Coaster Ride, on the other hand, starts with a quick rise fueled by high expectations, followed with sharp ups and downs due to increased volatility, and finally a sudden drop followed by a prolonged decline.

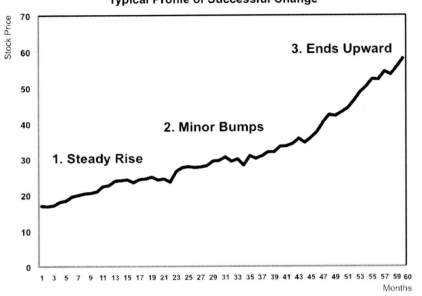

The Path of Ascent
Typical Profile of Successful Change

Change Masters

Unfortunately, most companies opt for the Roller Coaster Ride, hoping to make change happen, even if it's not good. Even many of those who have at one point been on the Path of Ascent may not remain on track permanently. For some, their initial successes have led to overconfidence, arrogance, and, ultimately, poor choices. Before they know it, they are riding the roller coaster. An increasing number of people and organizations have entered into this cycle, experiencing the pattern of failed change.

A casual breakfast conversation with the CEO of a company that did not change successfully illustrates the point. "I'm not sure what went wrong. We were making progress. I was spending my entire energy telling my leaders how to run the organization better. But the direct approach that got us going at first could not sustain performance in the end," he frankly explained. "If you had to do it over again," I asked him, "what would you do differently?" He responded, "I would definitely pay more attention to the culture."

The Roller Coaster Ride
Typical Profile of Change Failure

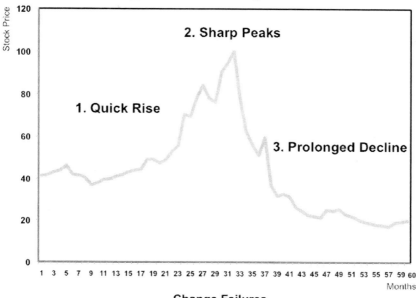

Change Failures

Culture is a vital component behind all successful change, and the CEO was referring to culture particularly as it relates to gaining people's commitment to change. When looking at the successful changes, I noticed that even when the initial leadership decisions were bold and often controversial, the leaders were able to earn the trust and loyalty of their employees, thus also earning the employees' commitment to change.

Companies that fail to change never reach such commitment. Leaders at these companies try to impose change on others. Employees, in turn, see their leaders as the primary cause for failure. People at these organizations end up expecting others to change, often blaming others for the disappointing results.

The Roller Coaster Ride, when boiled down to its essence, is a mechanical process of trying to make others do what we want in order to get what we want. We may attempt to mandate change, covertly manipulate situations, or explicitly motivate others with incentives. But in the end, we cannot change others, no matter what we do. The Roller Coaster Ride approach is doomed to fail.

Comparing the Change Masters with the Change Failures, one can easily discern the difference. The Five Ascent Principles stand in stark contrast with the five opposing forces that cause change to fail. A quick description highlights the key differences between the Path of Ascent and the Roller Coaster Ride.

Common Purpose vs. Lack of Trust

On the Path of Ascent, a shared vision of success binds people to a common cause, helping them overcome internal differences and external adversity. As people contribute to their story of success, they increase their capacity to create the envisioned future.

On the Roller Coaster Ride, people distrust other's motives, often second guessing their agendas and protecting their interests. There are divisions, turf battles, and a pervasive "us and them" attitude. Lack of trust breeds defensive behaviors that delay results and play out worst-case scenarios.

Clear Direction vs. Lack of Focus

On the Path of Ascent, people openly discuss what needs to be done. They listen to feedback to clarify objectives and make informed decisions. People understand their role in the overall game plan. The organization is agile at seizing opportunities for change.

On the Roller Coaster Ride, leaders set targets without fully understanding the situation. Their mandates create competing priorities and confusion. People stick to what is more familiar, avoid risks, and make poor decisions. The organization attempts to pursue too many initiatives at once.

Building on Strengths vs. Poor Capability

On the Path of Ascent, talent is placed where it is most vitally needed. An objective view of people's strengths determines who does what. People are constantly learning and taking on progressive challenges. The organization builds on strengths by consistently attracting, promoting, and developing each member's talents.

On the Roller Coaster Ride, position rather than capacity dictates who does what. People are kept in roles that may not be their best fit, thus blocking others from progressing. People focus on putting out fires and areas needing improvement rather than on strengths. The organization grows complacent and tolerant of poor behavior.

Teamwork and Collaboration vs. Weak Commitment

On the Path of Ascent, people work as a team to reach peak performance. They collaborate with each other inside and outside their immediate team, projecting widespread success. Work becomes intrinsically motivating as it taps into personal drivers of engagement. The organization creates the conditions where the best people can consistently excel.

On the Roller Coaster Ride, interaction between departments and functions is transactional. There is a pervasive sense that the company doesn't always act in the best interest of the employees, so employees, in turn, work by the contract. People rely on rules, policies and regulations to define what to do. Discretionary effort is limited.

Increasing Progress vs. Delayed Results

On the Path of Ascent, the focus is on results. Performance measures are tracked regularly to report progress toward well-defined goals. People talk openly about accountabilities, deadlines, and project status. Significant gains are achieved incrementally through continuous improvements.

On the Roller Coaster Ride, the focus is on activity. People are required to attend lengthy review meetings. It is unclear who is ultimately responsible for doing what. Reports are "to do" lists describing tasks and actions. When goals are not met, people point to circumstances out of their control.

```
┌─────────────────────────────────────────┐
│                                         │
│              Improving                  │
│          from the inside out            │
│            changes us and               │
│           our destination.              │
│                                         │
└─────────────────────────────────────────┘
```

What is the difference between these two paths? The Path
of Ascent is the result of a sincere desire to change by acting on
principles. The focus is on getting better, not on changing others
or the situation. The Path of Ascent is a change from the inside
out that changes us and our destination.

There is no such thing as organizational change. There is
only personal change. Our change influences others and collectively, our actions change organizations.

Making the Right Choice

The intent behind the change is critical. How we go about
changing is even more important than what we are to change. A
reorganization of your team, for example, is not necessarily good
or bad. How you go about reorganizing your team, however, has
consequences for everyone in your team. As a result of how you
change, your team can become weaker or stronger. In the process, you must address five key questions.

1. As you make decisions . . .
   a. Are people able to trust your motives?
   b. Or do they question your intentions?

2. As you set priorities . . .
   a. Are you helping people reassess what they do?
   b. Or are you imposing conflicting directions?

3. As you increase efficiency . . .
   a. Are you removing unnecessary work?
   b. Or are you cutting core capabilities?

4. As you strive to become more effective . . .
    a. Are you keeping people engaged?
    b. Or are you sacrificing long-term commitment?

5. As you lead change . . .
    a. Are you getting results from the start?
    b. Or are you taking a long time before seeing success?

If your answer for each of these questions is (a), you are leading your team on the Path of Ascent. On the other hand, if you answer one or more of these questions with (b), you and your team are likely riding the Roller Coaster.

HOW we change is as important as WHAT we change.

How we change is as important as *what* we change. The change process itself reveals important cues determining the odds for success or failure. Success leaves foot prints that if correctly followed lead to more success. So does failure. By tracing the path you are on, you can recognize if the initiative is likely to succeed or fail.

"What if our organization is following both paths at once? Even our senior leaders represent both camps," commented a senior healthcare executive during a break after my conference presentation. His organization was in the midst of integrating several hospital acquisitions into the dominant host culture. "What then is our likely outcome?" he asked me pointedly.

"The outcomes will reflect the dominant side," I responded. Staring at me with a nervous smile, this senior executive concluded, "Our best chance then is to win some key people over to the ascent side." I nodded in agreement. We both realized the impact individual choices have on the end result.

The outcome of a change initiative—large or small—hinges on which path we take, not on the tools, processes, and systems we use to change. External conditions may accelerate or delay change, but they can't control the ultimate outcome. As individuals we decide what approach to change we take. For individuals and organizations, successful change is simply a choice.

Where are you heading right now? And, more importantly, how can you get on the Path of Ascent? Your fate and that of many others hang on which road you take. This choice makes all the difference. Destiny is a matter of choice.

We must become the change we want to see happen.

~ Mahatma Gandhi

In pursuit of ascent, we will learn how to get off the Roller Coaster Ride and get on the Path of Ascent. In chapter two we will walk right into momentous meetings at Sony Pictures and at a Nissan subsidiary that became the turning point in their downward course. In chapter three, we will get on the Path of Ascent as we follow Tom James from teaching leadership principles to applying those same principles in leading a remarkable turnaround at Crown Packaging, a Canadian paper company on the verge of a crisis.

The middle section of this book, chapters four through eight, give us a full appreciation of how the Five Ascent Principles work in our jobs and in our lives. We will visit the Change Masters companies, going from the boardroom to the field operations, and observing up-close how the Five Ascent Principles gave them a definitive edge. As we course through leadership styles, management decisions, and corporate cultures at these exemplary companies, we will take an occasional look at the comparison companies that did not make the Change Masters list and see how they fell short.

The third section of this book is about practical applications for modern workplaces. In chapter nine we put together the Ascent process, walking with Wayne and Joanne, ordinary people who applied the Five Ascent Principles to change their lives, teams, and organizations for the better. In the concluding chapter, we will recount how, even in the worst of times and all around the world, people and organizations have applied the Five Ascent Principles to turn near certain failure into outstanding and lasting success.

All change is not growth, as all movement is not forward.

~ Ellen Glasgow

## CHAPTER TWO

Getting off the Roller Coaster

The easier it is to do, the harder it is to change.

~Eng's Principle

Growth Is Optional

In a time when risks, costs, and competition are reaching peak levels, changing successfully becomes crucial. With a growing emphasis on timely results, people can no longer afford to initiate a change and simply hope it works. Neither can they wait or delay action until conditions become more favorable. Yet too many initiatives end up producing disappointing results. The first step to eliminate these growing challenges is to understand why changes so often fail.

Early in my consulting career, I was invited to attend a crucial meeting with the executive team at Sony Pictures in Culver City, California. As I walked into the meeting, I was met by Larry, the senior partner of the prominent consulting firm Sony Pictures had engaged in a major change initiative. He walked up to me and whispered into my ear: "Change is inevitable. You're lucky to be here."

Then Larry looked into my eyes and stated, "Your job here is to watch and listen—not to speak. After the meeting, we can talk about it." I didn't know how to respond, so I just looked back at him. He read my hesitation and cracked a big smile. Putting his arm around my shoulders, he simply said: "You'll make a good consultant someday. Have you ever thought about joining our firm?" Larry left me with that thought as he went on to greet the others.

The work I was doing with Sony Pictures was my first big break as an independent consultant. Less than a year before, I had decided to leave the consulting firm I was working with to launch my own consulting practice. This prominent client represented my entire livelihood, and as Larry noted, it was a lucky break for my career. I had been contracted to facilitate the cultural change. During the six months leading up to this meeting I had become well acquainted with the issues and the players involved in this change.

The tension between departments and functions at Sony Pictures had been building steadily for months in anticipation of this meeting. After hearing many disconcerting stories—part fact, part fiction—the heads of the different business divisions had come together to assess the actual progress of a massive reorganization of their worldwide operations.

The consultants came well prepared with heavy artillery: senior partners, practice area experts, and vast amounts of data. Sony's senior managers lined up in different camps based on which side of the issue they fell. A high-ranking officer, Mr. Yazaki, had come from Japan to oversee the change initiative. The stakes were high, with millions of dollars, hundreds of jobs, promising careers, and customer relationships depending on the meeting's outcome. The simple question that called for the meeting was: "Is the change working?"

I can't remember much of what was said during the meeting that led to my critical moment. I sat at the large conference room table listening to the consultants' presentation and to the questions and answers that followed. I was caught up in observing the dynamics, when suddenly Mr. Yazaki pointed his finger directly at me and asked, "What do you think?"

There was total silence. I felt all eyes fixed on me, especially Larry's. I was a total outsider to both the company and the consulting firm. Without even thinking, I responded, "I don't think it will work." Even as I spoke the words, I realized the implications of what I was saying.

Larry immediately jumped in saying. "What Juan meant is that at present, there is not sufficient evidence to . . ." Mr. Yazaki gestured with his hand for Larry to stop, and then asked me another question: "Why not?"

I explained to Mr. Yazaki and the entire executive staff that there was little commitment in support of the change among the executives and even less commitment among the employees. I pointed out that in order to succeed, the change required greater collaboration among the key players and broader support from the employees.

The rest is a blur: the intense discussions during the meeting, the severe criticisms and chastisement right after the meeting for speaking out of line with my role in the project, the many messages on my answering machine the next morning, the political maneuvers in the weeks following, and the eventual repercussions from that eventful meeting—all fused in a tumult of words and emotions.

Nine months later, Sony Pictures announced a change of direction. New executives replaced the former ones. The contract with the consulting firm came to an end. Those who had invested emotionally and otherwise in the former initiative had to realign their loyalties, while others rejoiced triumphantly. Needless to say, I never received a job offer from Larry—but I did continue working with Sony.

From 1999 to 2003 Sony's transformation efforts were focused internally on improving operational efficiency, cutting costs, and reorganizing management. The customer was not in the picture. Neither was there full buy-in from employees across different business units. Delayed results and less-than-compelling leadership resulted in superficial cost reductions. But midway through the process, leaders at Sony Pictures recognized the error and corrected it, still in time to avoid a total disaster and reverse a negative trend. Sony Pictures put its pride aside, cut its losses, and got off the Roller Coaster Ride.

Seven out of ten Change Masters were in dire need of getting off their Roller Coaster Rides. Their Path of Ascent began with the realization that they could no longer continue the way they were going. Their first step, no matter how painful or embarrassing, was getting off the wrong course. It is far better to admit a fault than to stubbornly persevere on the wrong path. The challenge lies in being able to recognize when an approach is fundamentally flawed.

Most leaders would consider making a U-turn mid course quitting too early, giving up under pressure, or being easily swayed by public opinion. On the other hand, a wise person knows when to admit to a fault and change. How can we discern in the heat of the moment the difference between abandoning a course simply because of its difficulty, and having the wisdom to recognize a fundamental error in our approach?

The difference lies in discerning between trying to prove our point—requiring others to change, or finding the point—and ascending. As long as the focus is on who is right, we can't clearly see what is right. The desire to search for what is right regardless of where the solutions originate is the first step toward getting off the Roller Coaster Ride.

Choosing what is right regardless of consequences is the key to making any type of improvement. What got the Change Masters off the Roller Coaster and onto the Path of Ascent was their capacity to put what needs to be done above personal egos and set agendas. The Change Failures did not get off the Roller Coaster and stubbornly continued on their course.

**Focusing on *what* is right
rather than on *who* is right
gets us off the Roller
Coaster Ride.**

Change is inevitable.

Growth is optional.

In recognizing the need for a fundamental change, I readily concur with Larry's comment: "Change is inevitable." One way or the other, things are going to change. But growth, the positive side of change is far from inevitable. It is, in fact, entirely optional.

Accepting the need for making a U-turn takes courage, especially after having made a significant investment—financially and emotionally. But the alternative is far worse. We cannot get on the Path of Ascent unless we first get off the Roller Coaster Ride. The good news is that the relief of getting on the right track is immediate. We begin by assessing where a change is headed.

The best way to break a bad habit is to drop it.

~Leo Aikman

Identifying Widening Gaps

Where do we start? An assessment of current practices helps us identify a pattern of conduct leading to a predictable outcome. To the extent a work group is caught on the Roller Coaster, there is a need to make a U-turn, at least in some areas. Abandoning ineffective practices, replacing poor habits, and discarding faulty assumptions provide the starting point for the Ascent. To the extent a group is on the Path of Ascent, there is great value to pointing out and reinforce the root causes for their continuing success.

An introspective assessment provides the basis for identifying current strengths and challenges. Conduct a quick assessment with a specific group of people in mind. It can be a large functional department or a small team. Identify to which extent each of the traits on the following page apply to this work group.

Ascent Profile
Linking People with Results

Overall Performance	Very Poor	Poor	Fair	Well	Very Well	Excellent
Build Common Purpose • Shared Vision • Customer Focus • Trust in Coworkers • Stakeholder Alignment	Very Poor	Poor	Fair	Well	Very Well	Excellent
Clarify Direction • Evaluate Priorities • Set Concrete Goals • Define Responsibilities • Delegate Effectively	Very Poor	Poor	Fair	Well	Very Well	Excellent
Develop Capacity • Right Person for the Job • Required Resources • Open Communications • Process Improvement	Very Poor	Poor	Fair	Well	Very Well	Excellent
Inspire Commitment • Collaboration • Teamwork • Recognition • Rewards	Very Poor	Poor	Fair	Well	Very Well	Excellent
Achieve Results • Results Focus • Customer Feedback • Performance Measures • Accountability	Very Poor	Poor	Fair	Well	Very Well	Excellent

The Ascent Profile evaluates current performance on five key areas and links them to predictable outcomes. As you review the results of the Ascent Profile, you will indentify high and low marks pointing to the root causes of current performance. These scores may simply reflect the tip of the iceberg. To improve on what is currently happening; focus on building strengths and overcoming challenges. The objective is to achieve better results by improving your performance.

What are the team's greatest strengths? Not every team excels in every aspect. Understanding where your team excels provides the anchor for further improvement. It is common to underestimate the value of strengths in facilitating continuing growth. Take the time to recognize and reinforce what you are already doing well. It is by applying our strengths that we make our greatest contributions.

What areas need the most improvement? Often, team members are not fully aware of how their deficiencies impact the team. Deficiencies, in general, are a drag pulling us down. When a deficiency is pronounced it can become a derailer, keeping us from reaching our full potential. Take the time to identify and correct deficiencies to make a U-turn and get on the right track.

All change starts with the awareness that we are not where we want to be. Increased perception is the trigger for realizing a fundamental need for change. As we realize that the current course will not lead us to the desired results, we can stop perpetuating a negative trend.

> **All change starts
> with the awareness
> that we are not
> where we want to be.**

The number of companies successfully managing change has increased just slightly, while the number reporting limited or no success has risen by 60%. These organizations rate their ability to manage change a full 22% lower than their expected need for it. This represents a "change gap" that has widened by 14% between 2006 and 2008. The gap between our need to change and our ability to manage it has almost tripled in only two years![4]

Our capacity to change with changing times is becoming a matter of survival. Our ability to change is improving at a much slower rate than the pace of change. In order to seize the opportunities and minimize the risks, we as individuals, teams, and organizations need to learn how to change successfully. We need to overcome the negative tendencies that limit our capacity to ascend.

It is not the strongest of the species that survives, nor the most intelligent, but the one most responsive to change.

~Charles Darwin

After concluding a day's training on leadership and organizational change, I had dinner with a group of participants representing large corporations. They were exchanging stories of change at their own organizations. Their comments left me, their trainer and consultant, stunned and searching for answers.

"We are required by the Securities and Exchange Commission to give proof of increased transparency and ethical conduct of the top 2,000 leaders through open communication and 360-degree feedback. The survey results are so high that we suspect the managers are gaming the system."

"We have had five CEOs in three years. The last three left even before communicating a direction for our company. The most recent one lasted only three months before taking a different job. The current one is coming from Asia, and after six months has not yet been a single day in his office in the U.S."

"Just for our entry level jobs at the call center we are requiring college graduates with good grades. All others just don't have the knowledge or skills these jobs now demand. Besides, there are plenty of well educated people available around the world."

"I've been asked to take the lead in my organization because we had so many people leave. After only eighteen months I am the most senior person in the group! I told my manager I was not sure I wanted the job. She told me she was not sure she wanted hers either."

"After three years of process reengineering, and an army of consultants, our company is no better off. Everything is a mess. Now, the old process is broken and the new one doesn't work well yet. They say more investment is necessary to solve it."

As we considered the waste, confusion, and dysfunction resulting from these situations, one of the participants at the table summed up the conversation: *"Change is no longer the issue. We take change for granted. The real issue now is how can we benefit from change?"*

Implied in these statements is the realization that change is leaving substantial and lasting negative effects. To some extent, some downside from change is inevitable. Pain can result from any situation requiring people to adjust to shifting conditions. Yet, much of the waste, confusion, and anguish we are struggling with are avoidable.

The most prevalent problems that hinder progress are low trust, lack of focus, poor capability, weak commitment, and delayed results. These are the key areas that create five widening gaps between needed change and actual improvement. The trend shows a steady widening of these gaps, as the magnitude of the problems increases faster than our ability to deal with them.

The Five Widening Gaps	
Low Trust	Low trust caused by corruption, greed, and unethical conduct
Lack of Focus	Lack of focus due to too many initiatives and competing priorities
Poor Capability	Poor capability by not having the talent needed for the position
Weak Commitment	Weak commitment due to inconsistent leadership and poor example
Delayed Results	Delayed results from low accountability and lack of discipline to follow through

You may recognize how one or several of these widening gaps are affecting people where you work. You may also notice that your personal life is impacted by these gaps as well. To the extent we see these problems spread in society, at work, and at home, we will continue to struggle creating desirable change.

More importantly, if we identify any of these widening gaps in our personal lives, we must realize our contribution to the problem. Since all change starts with individuals, we must learn to recognize and correct negative tendencies in ourselves first. A better understanding of the problem will help us know how to effectively resolve it.

Low Trust

By far the biggest challenge in organizations is low trust. This widening gap has compromising integrity at its root. From the well-publicized scandals of fraud among the higher levels of leadership at some of the largest organizations, to the everyday broken promises and tainted truths of rank-and-file employees, organizations suffer from decreasing trust. This decline is measurable. A 2005 Harris poll reveals that a substantial majority of Americans (55%) and Europeans (63%) distrust their governments. Only 22% of Americans trust the media, and about 1 in 10 Americans trust big companies.

From the time of Enron's landmark bankruptcy in 2001, that implicated one of the world's top accounting firms, Arthur Andersen, trillions of dollars have been intentionally stolen through institutionalized accounting fraud and legal corruption. The financial cost of corruption in America and worldwide is huge. The underlying effects on society are devastating and virtually incalculable. As investors and the general public have lost confidence in once reputable institutions and social contracts, vast sums of value have vanished. These practices represent a crime affecting all levels of our society.

Less obvious but just as damaging is how interpersonal trust is broken by not fulfilling one's promises, or not doing one's best at a job. When a manager goes back on decisions, hides uncomfortable news, or plays office politics for personal convenience, others will begin to distrust. These seemingly minor faults deeply affect relationships, often beyond recovery. People who fail to keep simple promises not only lose others' trust, but also lack self respect.

In addition to intentional wrongdoing, many people breed distrust at the workplace simply by playing out their justifiable fears. Insecurities about one's employment, job relevance, or performance have turned many peers into competitors. Emotional withholding and verbal attacks have turned team interactions into a mine field. Ironically, the fear to speak openly and respectfully about others furthers dysfunction and distrust.

Lack of Focus

The best ideas and the greatest plans often fall apart in the fog of execution. We live in a fast-paced society, increasingly characterized by impulsiveness, hyperactivity, and inattention. We are so busy "doing" that we fail to focus long enough to do anything particularly well. Lack of focus is a main cause why smart people do dumb things. Being busy does not mean accomplishing more. When we work at a frantic pace, we often make more mistakes. In the rush to get a lot of urgent tasks done, we frequently miss out on doing what matters most right.

Hyperactivity reflects the need for constant motion—being unable to pause and sit still. Even when it is time to rest, some report that they need a vacation from their vacation, as the time that was intended for relaxation ends up being busier than the regular work routine. Hyperactivity leads to chronic fatigue, depression, and mental illness. Our society consumes increasingly higher doses of antidepressants to cope with hyperactive disorders.

Lack of focus is the most prevalent leadership flaw, manifesting itself in companies having too many initiatives, competing priorities, and conflicting directions. This problem is magnified by economic uncertainty. Companies going through tough times often respond to unpredictable situations by panicking. They try to do more with less, rather than simplifying and becoming more focused.

Lacking clear direction, these organizations pursue too many opportunities and fail to deliver strong results in any one area.

They become reactive instead of charting a coherent course. They spread their resources across a myriad of evolving opportunities, hoping that at least some will be successful. The result is a thin layer of investment and activity spread across too many initiatives, without a clear focus on anything in particular.

Some organizations, in search of direction, hire leaders from outside the company, hoping that the outsider will bring a fresh perspective and show them the way. Unfortunately, these frequent shifts at the helm further disorient the organization, leaving thousands of employees going in disparate directions. Confused and frustrated, many employees opt to take no responsibility for the organization's course.

Employees, overwhelmed by multiple and competing demands, jump into overdrive. They feel powerless to renegotiate priorities, clarify assignments, or question initiatives. Instead of focusing, they nod in agreement to incoming directions and hope against reason to meet at least some of their goals. When the crazy-busy working mode becomes chronic, many resort to passive-aggressive behaviors to cope with the stress.

Poor Capability

More than ever before, what a person can or cannot do defines his or her future opportunities. The amount of education and skills a person has dictates how much others think that person's job is worth. The battle for talent is now waged globally as companies selectively pick highly educated and skilled workers from anywhere. The nations, communities, and companies that are most successful in developing human talent, particularly college-level knowledge and specialized skills, enjoy significant advantages.

There is a growing need for higher education for getting any decent job. In the United States, this perception has increased from 31% in 2000 to 50% in 2007. Ongoing learning and advanced education are essential to successful employment. Emerging nations like India and China are outproducing the United States in terms of actual numbers of people with advanced education. With 16 million people enrolled in higher education, China is already producing a substantial share of the world's science and engineering graduates each year—three times the number of engineers graduating in the United States. India is not far behind, with approximately 9 million students in higher education.[5]

In terms of quality of education, Canadian and American universities consistently rank among the best in the world. But other countries are quickly catching up with centers of excellence that are world renowned. India's elite science and technology institutes, for example, rank among the world's best, producing graduates who take leading posts in national and multinational firms.[6]

The United States is still among the top nations in the proportion of older adults holding a college degree, but the United States drops to seventh place in the educational attainment of young adults ages 25 to 34. For most of the 1990s, the United States ranked last among 14 industrialized nations in raising college participation rates.[7] Part of the problem is that high school education in the United States is deficient. In a survey of over 400 organizations, the Society for Human Resources Management (SHRM) found that over 42% say that high school graduates entering the workforce are "deficient" in overall preparation for entry-level jobs, primarily in written English, math, reading comprehension, critical thinking and problem solving, and work ethic.[8]

Making this problem worse, many companies respond to economic downturns by cutting training and development budgets. Doing away with training may provide a temporary financial relief, at a long-term cost on capability. Thirty-nine percent of North American firms are concerned with their ability to transfer knowledge to younger workers and to bring new employees up to speed.[9]

Ironically, when it matters most, people don't necessarily do their best. Instead of becoming more productive, many employees respond to uncertainty by protecting their jobs. The best qualified person does not always get the job. It's more who you know than what you know. In some cases, key positions are filled with people who know how to play the system. Aware of competitive talent vying for their position, they hold on to their jobs by blocking access to new talent, limiting the organization's capacity to grow. Ultimately, individuals who don't keep pace with the rising worldwide educational standards will find their economic future at stake.

Weak Commitment

Commitment is another widening gap in today's society and it manifests in the workplace as low engagement. Many leaders see a deteriorating work ethic for which they are in part responsible. The social contract between employers and employees has been compromised in the mindless pursuit of profits. As a result, working relationships at all levels are becoming more transactional.

Adding to decreasing commitment is an increasingly more transient workforce. The U.S. Bureau of Labor Statistics (BLS) tracking the U.S. workforce between 1979 and 1994 shows that 36% of jobs ended in less than a year, and 72% ended in fewer than five years due to turnover. The typical U.S. worker held an average of 10.5 jobs between ages 18 and 40, not counting promotions within the same company. Occupations such as food preparation and healthcare services have even shorter periods of employment, averaging 22 months on the job. For an increasing number of people, jobs are a revolving door, in one day, out another.

Commitment to the worker is also low by the organization. Employees are increasingly more reluctant to commit to an organization that has a track record of not being loyal to them. This weakening commitment is seldom verbalized directly, as it has become expected at many organizations, but it is manifested in numerous uncooperative behaviors. The most common is when departments and functions hold back information instead of collaborating with each other.

Because of divisions within the organizations, leaders often run into problems when they ask their workforce to make sacrifices. Change efforts become political because commitment exists only within rival camps. Employees in a divided organization cannot engage in a productive way.

The role of the immediate supervisor is essential for fostering commitment in workers. Immediate supervisors represent the company to the employee. Their conduct reflects the organization's standard. When a supervisor fails to lead employees in a way that inspires teamwork and collaboration, commitment falters. If a supervisor over controls the staff, the best workers usually leave. The most common problem affecting morale is when supervisors don't provide sincere recognition—a key driver of employee engagement. Less than half of the time, supervisors give heartfelt praise for a job well done. This simple action costs nothing and takes little time to do, and yet it is a crucial component in engaging a workforce. Companies unable to engage their employees cannot enlist their commitment to change.[10]

Delayed Results

About 70% of major organizational change efforts fail to deliver the expected results. The leading indicator of failed outcomes is the lack of initial results. Many promising initiatives become prematurely aborted due to failure to show short-term gains. Insufficient attention to short term results kills even the best strategies and change plans.

Low accountability is the main source for delayed results. When people realize they are not likely to make a goal, rather than analyzing what went wrong and make corrections, they opt for the easier approach. They blame others. There are plenty of excuses for not being able to meet one's goal, but none of them compensate for the failure to deliver. Mangers are expected to hold others accountable, but they often fail to hold themselves accountable to their staff. The staff mimics their leader, shrugging off responsibility, therefore rendering the entire team unaccountable for results.

Under pressure to show early gains, some people orchestrate "quick wins" simply by playing the system. Anyone can make the numbers say almost anything to show results. But, without credible evidence of improvement, fabricated results backfire and create subsequent resistance to change. If initial successes are not legitimate, they substantially hinder real progress.

Upfront investment is often played as an excuse for poor evidence of progress. Some change initiatives claim that before producing tangible gains months of upfront planning and organizing are required. After much investment, however, most of these change initiatives still show no clear results. To be successful an organization must balance the short and the long term. Achieving early wins builds support for pursuing longer term goals. Successful change starts by producing early signs of success.[11]

The chains of habit are generally too small to be felt until they are too strong to be broken.

~Samuel Johnson

Closing the Gaps

Can you recognize some of these gaps in your organization? Many will readily admit to at least a few of these gaps, if not most of them. To the extent that these gaps do exist in your organization, you are riding the Roller Coaster at work. These gaps explain why change initiatives fail.

Do these gaps exist in our immediate work groups and close relationships? How much these gaps permeate our relationships can determine if we will realize our goals. Our ability to establish fulfilling and productive relationships depends on our capacity to help each other achieve our growth potential.

Some of the significant problems we experience are not growing pains, but the result of poor choices. These problems are unnecessary, correctible, and avoidable. Ineffective choices, attitudes, and behaviors persist in our work organizations and in the societies where we live, and these negative traits seem to be spreading like a virus and at an epidemic rate.

We cannot accept today's mistakes and failures in managing change as normal. Instead, we must stand up to these challenges. Our problems are avoidable—there is an alternative route. They are also curable—we can identify their root causes and replace them with something better. We have examples before us, including those presented in this book, showing how these gaps can be closed. The quality of our future depends on our choices today.

Business cannot succeed in a world that fails.

~Bertrand Collomb

## CHAPTER THREE

Getting on the Path of Ascent

*I know of no more encouraging fact than
the unquestionable ability of man to elevate
his life by conscious endeavor.*

~Henry David Thoreau

Beating the Odds

Hans looked at Tom straight in the eye and with great sincerity posed the question: "If you believe what you just told us, why don't you apply these principles to lead this group? Put your money where your mouth is and prove this theory. Rather than just talk about it, make it work."[12]

Tom had been wishing for such an opportunity for quite some time. Now that it was right in front of him, he was not so sure it was such a great idea after all. Accepting the challenge required a significant commitment to actually apply the principles he had been teaching for many years.

Besides, the company's situation was a real mess. Laden with debt and facing a market downturn, nothing short of an amazing turnaround would save the company. Tom also realized that he would need vast support since he knew nothing about the industry. Finally, Tom, a natural entrepreneur, had never worked for anyone else before. "Could I do it?" he wondered, but after some consideration, Tom accepted the job as chief operating officer at Crown Packaging.

Hans, the son of German immigrants, had come to Canada hoping to study medicine and become a doctor. But an accident that seriously injured his father changed Hans's plans for his future. He found a job to support his family. He began working on the floor of a local paper plant. Soon he began moving up the management ranks by making noticeable contributions to the operations.

After gaining some experience, Hans decided to pool all of his savings and, with Tim Dwane as a partner, he purchased a small plant that produced corrugated cardboard boxes. Operations flourished, and it didn't take long before Hans and Tim began expanding their business by opening new locations and buying out existing competitors. Hans, in particular, had little hesitation in letting the company grow as quickly as possible, even though both partners were taking sizable financial risks. In a remarkable 10-year period, the two entrepreneurs developed Crown Packaging, a vertically integrated paper company based in Western Canada that produced in excess of $350 million in annual revenue.

During the period of Crown's rapid expansion, which lasted through the early 1990s, the market was strong, credit was easily available, and Wall Street analysts projected solid growth. However, just one year after completing the acquisitions, the economy took a dramatic downturn. Crown ended with over a half billion dollars in debt and massive interest payments due on a strict schedule. The company was far from performing well enough to make those payments, especially during a market decline. Crown executives realized that the company could not pay off its debt load unless they made a drastic change.[13]

At this point, Hans invited Tom, who had been consulting with Crown's leaders, to present a proposal for improving the operations. Tom gave his all during the presentation, bluntly delivering his assessment and recommendations. "Crown needs to make a quantum leap without additional capital. It will require everyone's full effort to pull it off." Tom paused before concluding, "Someone at this table has got to lead this company. Leadership cannot be delegated." As he finished, he noticed he was shivering. The room fell silent. Hans, staring at each of the players around the table, intuitively sensed that Tom was the one for the job.

The first and most telling sign that Crown's turnaround was likely to succeed became evident at that initial meeting. Hans knew, almost instinctively, that someone who was personally committed to the cause had to lead the initiative. He couldn't do it himself, and neither could any of his senior executives. He wisely recognized their talents, roles, and contributions; and leading change was not among of them. Hans needed someone who could lead change by example, someone who could demonstrate by word and action what needed to be done.

> # Leading by example
> # cannot be delegated.

Whether you lead a large organization, a small team, or simply your own family, your role as a leader cannot be delegated. One of the most difficult challenges of leadership is that it requires your example. The group generally rises no higher than the example of their leader. If you ever feel frustrated that others are not embracing change, take a good look at yourself. Chances are good that you are not either.

Back to Crown's story. We will walk with Tom into his dream job. His welcome party was more like a nightmare. Upon arrival to the job, Tom received news of a worker fatality. Apparently, a maintenance employee who had been repairing the gigantic paper mill had disregarded safety rules. He accidentally tripped, fell into the machine, and went through the rollers that turn pulp into paper.

In addition, distrust between labor and management was rampant, and there were rumors of a union strike. Much of the workforce blamed management for the company's situation and would not be easily persuaded to change their views, much less cooperate with the culprit.

Hans, recognizing that his drive to build Crown had placed everyone in a precarious financial situation, talked openly with the workers about the situation. While Hans was focused on his company's success, he never forgot where he came from, and he felt responsible for all the employees that counted on him for their livelihood. He talked openly with the workers about the situation and the need for their support. Most felt his sincerity.

As if conditions were not bleak enough, the company's creditors encouraged Crown to file for bankruptcy. The creditors doubted that Crown would come through, so they were anxious to recover at least part of their investment. One of the general managers summed up the sentiment at the time: "Don't get us wrong, Tom. We're willing to try anything at this point. Let's just say, however, that we share some healthy skepticism."

Sure enough, Crown needed to reduce costs and improve productivity, but more importantly, the company needed a new mindset—a vision of a better future. Tom led the management team in creating a shared vision for Crown, which they called "The Bridge to Success." The visual representation illustrated change as a bridge suspended by cables—the key initiatives— and supported by pillars—the company's mission, vision, and values. As a clear reminder of the danger involved in crossing the bridge, the graphic portrayed sharks in the water with labels: *uncertainty, complacency, competition,* and *cycles (of debt payment).*

Within a few months, Tom assembled a team of high caliber and talented individuals from inside and outside the organization. The management lineup included well known people in the paper industry. I was brought in to assist in the change effort by coaching the senior leaders, providing employee feedback, and training the managers.

Each of Crown's newly formed divisions had worked as independent businesses, never truly coming together after their

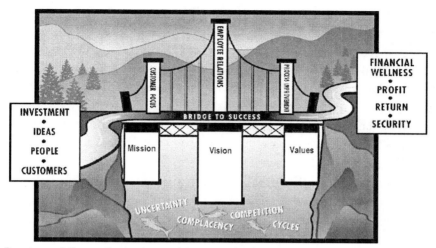

Courtesy of Crown Packaging archives. Leadership Instincts, Tom James

acquisition. Competition and distrust among division managers was so great that even scheduling a meeting proved difficult. Mangers from the different divisions embodied conflicting philosophies and saw little value in collaboration.

Tom started personally teaching leadership principles. Training hardly seemed like a sound investment of time and energy given the many pressing needs at the time, but it proved essential to their success. "Talking about principles got us to start thinking win-win," explained one of the division leaders. "We recognized the importance of telling our employees where the business was going. We needed their full support, hands, hearts, and minds," commented another general manager.[14] Others concurred that leadership principles became the catalyst for becoming a united group able to tackle their phenomenal challenges.

Out of necessity the group of executives began to work as a team. They realized that the company's overall well-being depended on looking beyond their own divisions' interests. As they started seeing the bigger picture, they realized what they could accomplish if they worked together. As the leaders became united, the employees working for them also began to collaborate.

Without additional cash available, improvements had to come from creative use of existing assets—mainly the creative ideas of the employees. In order to develop and engage the workforce, Tom organized a cross-divisional Strategic Implementation team charged with implementing quality methods. The SI team, as it became known, went to the different divisions, starting with the ones needing the most help, and trained the workers while working alongside with them until the workers were able to continue their own process improvements.

Members of militant Canadian unions, accustomed to the labor bargaining process, were asked to embrace a collaborative approach to schedules and wages. Supporting productivity improvements could mean going against one of their primary interests, namely, protecting union members' jobs. In the end, they realized that the only way to keep the company open was to work together, and the union leaders decided to trust that Hans would do what he could to protect jobs.

Hans reciprocated their vote of trust and continued to work under extremely tight financial conditions to preserve worker's jobs as much as possible. In the end, Crown's decision to close non-competitive operations resulted in minimal layoffs, but the company provided early retirement benefits and education and placement support to those who were laid off. The decision to protect jobs proved wise as the workforce responded by finding creative ways of making the operations more efficient in the long run.

Quarterly loan payments threatened to force the struggling company into bankruptcy. People throughout the organization stretched beyond their comfort zones to adopt new ideas, design new processes, and learn new skills—all of these changes happened at a fast pace and without assurance of ultimate success.

Beating the odds, Crown made a remarkable turnaround. A group of ordinary people pulled together to do the extraordinary under distressing conditions. In only three years, they were able to pay off the debt completely, improve quality, launch new products, and significantly increase profits. They did all this without capital investment or massive layoffs.

The nonfinancial results of Crown's turnaround are also impressive. Crown attracted new customers through more competitive products. Employees at all levels gained valuable skills, in some cases leading to important promotions. Division leaders, once industry rivals, became collaborative colleagues, and many of them went on to successful careers in other organizations. All who had at one point or another had been skeptical of the change process, eventually became staunch advocates, including the leader at the most improved division, who went on to start his own leadership coaching firm after his experience at Crown. One of the managers concluded, "Towards the end, we felt we were 10 feet tall and bullet proof."

How did they do it?

The Five Ascent Principles

A set of five principles provide the foundation for leading successful change. These principles were constantly present during the turnaround at Crown. Likewise, each of the Change Masters used these principles to lead their transformations. All stories of successful change, whether for organizations, teams, or individuals, show a distinctive pattern based on a consistent set of principles that I refer to as the Five Ascent Principles.

The following outline describes how to apply the Five Ascent Principles. Applying each individual principle helps achieve the corresponding outcome, such as increasing the team's purpose, direction, ability, motivation, and results. Applying the entire process takes the team to a higher level of performance.

Applying the Five Ascent Principles provides a comprehensive framework for mastering change. Suppose you are trying to improve your team's performance to become more efficient. The traditional approach would focus entirely on cutting costs, leaving it entirely up to the team's manager to make some tough decisions. The Ascent process provides an alternative to achieving a more sustainable gain. It starts by identifying the performance gaps with input from your team and other stakeholders. Once you fully understand the nature of the problem, you can facilitate the Ascent process described on the following page. Still, as a leader

The Ascent Plan
For Improving Team Performance

ENVISION: What do we want to see happen?
- Discuss the team's purpose—what is the team's mission and vision
- Describe the future success of the team
- Share the team's story of success with others
- Identify how the story of success will become real
  Outcome: Build Common Purpose

EVALUATE: How can we make it happen?
- Define the team's objectives
- Set concrete goals with measurable deadlines
- Assign specific responsibilities to each team member
- Create an action plan to achieve the objectives
  Outcome: Clarify Direction

EMPOWER: How do we build on strengths?
- Define the team's core competencies
- Link team members' strengths to the team's core competencies
- Decide how the team will develop the core competencies
- Define the process for the team to work more effectively
  Outcome: Develop Capacity

ENGAGE: How do we inspire collaboration?
- Discuss what engages peak performance in the team
- Identify how the team can create the conditions of engagement
- Facilitate collaboration and teamwork
- Provide coaching and feedback on individual performance
  Outcome: Inspire Commitment

EVOLVE: How do we track progress?
- Identify the results the team needs to achieve in the next 100 days
- Identify performance indicators for tracking progress
- Assign individuals to report on performance indicators
- Hold each other accountable for delivering results
  Outcome: Achieve Results

Access additional Ascent Tools at
www.ascent-advisor.com/tools.html

you will need to make some key decisions, but by involving your team, you can solve the problem in a way that it stays solved.

Crown's story describes the Five Ascent Principles at work. The Bridge to Success provided a shared vision of success in a time of uncertainty. Managers openly discussed the company's direction with all the employees, so everyone knew what had to be done. They deployed top talent in key roles while developing new skills and empowering the workforce. People learned to put differences aside and work as a team. Meanwhile, the focus on results was relentless, helping them achieve seemingly impossible goals.

The Five Ascent Principles can be seen clearly at each of the Change Masters. Behind the story of their success one can easily detect these principles at work. In some cases, they achieved a level of mastery of at least one or two of the principles. Personal experience working with client organizations, from executive teams to functional operations, confirms the consistent relevance of the Five Ascent Principles.

Conversely, these principles are not found, to any significant degree, in the stories of failed change. Going through the records and news articles documenting the transformation of the Change Failures, one quickly realizes that the Five Ascent Principles were not practiced. In fact, little or no attention was given to leading people because the focus was almost exclusively on managing change.

To see the specific connection between the use of the Five Ascent Principles at the Change Masters and the Change Failures, refer to the Appendix on page 215. It is important to note that while none of the changing organizations studied practiced these five principles to perfection, the difference between the Change Masters and the Change Failures is obvious.

For each principle we apply, we receive a direct and immediate benefit. The following section of this chapter provides a brief overview of each of the Five Ascent Principles. The following five chapters of this book explain each principle in greater detail with specific practices and examples for mastering change.

| 1 Envision | Create the story of success | Purpose |

Vision is the power to create the future. As we envision, we create the thoughts, words, and actions to produce what we want to happen. Our thoughts focus energy around an idea. Our words articulate what we are thinking. Words act as building blocks, creating a story that is ultimately carried out by our actions. Vision aligns our thoughts, words, and actions to produce what we want to create.

A successful future never just happened. It was created by diligently pursuing a compelling vision. Without vision, there is no purpose behind our actions. But with a clear vision we can bring the future to the present.

To be powerful, a vision needs to tell a story of the future. A team creates the story of success by describing how they will be. Using vivid images, describing ideal interactions, and pointing to desirable results, success stories move the team forward towards realizing their full potential.

Sharing the story of success is the best way to enlist others' help in creating the envisioned future. The story of success describes what we are after, enlisting others to be part of doing something great. They, in turn, become storytellers, actively sharing the story of success with others.

| 2 Evaluate | Seize the opportunity for change | Direction |

Change begins with a reality check. Sooner or later we all get a "wake up call" that helps us realize that we are not where we envisioned. Then we come to realize that our current path is not taking us where we want to go.

We sense the need for change as we experience the tension between the desired results and the current reality. This dissatisfaction grows to the point that we want to make an adjustment. The sense of urgency has to be sufficiently high for us to actually commit to modifying our behavior. While some people are more sensitive than others to this urge, eventually most people reach a critical point where they decide to make a change.

After the emotional commitment is made, we search for logical ways to make it happen. We use reason to decide how to change. At this point, we formulate the strategy—game plans to achieve our objective, set a target, and weigh risks and opportunities. Our resolve to change grows as we set a concrete plan of action, with steps and timelines, mapping our way forward.

| 3 | Empower | Develop capacity from strengths | Capacity |

Empowerment comes from using our strengths. We grow by leveraging existing strength to develop new capacity. In other words, we build on what is already working well to become even better. Building on a solid foundation, we can reach higher and broaden our skills.

We make the greatest contributions through our talents. Mastering talents takes deliberate practice, and there is no substitute for deliberate practice. If we are to grow, it is not enough merely to use a skill; we need to apply it to its fullest extent to make a difference. Our strengths, like a rising tent pole, elevate other related qualities.

In an organization, this means placing key players, the organization's best talent, where they can be most valuable now and in the future. Selecting the right person for the job is one of the most important tasks of a leader. The qualities of the person filling a key position affect the entire organization. We make the most of our human capital when we select, develop, and promote talented people to key positions in the organization.

| 4 | Engage | Inspire collaboration and teamwork | Commitment |

Engagement creates the conditions for peak performance. At the most basic level, what motivates others to change? When faced with risk and uncertainty, most people look for self preservation. They ask: "What's in it for me?" Overcoming resistance to change requires addressing people's basic needs.

Incentives, in the form of "carrots and sticks," though powerful motivators, work only in the short run. Sustained energy, productivity, quality, and commitment require engagement to achieve peak performance. Understanding what makes people thrive is essential to building high performing organizations.

Engagement is the voluntary dedication and commitment to doing our very best work. We are fully engaged when we apply our hearts and minds to what we do. When we choose to really invest personally in a cause greater than ourselves, we become fully engaged.

People are engaged by different aspects of a job, and the drivers of engagement may vary for a given group or organization. Leaders can build high performing organizations by creating the conditions that energize their people most.

Personal example is the most powerful tool to engage others. Nothing inspires more trust and collaboration than seeing a person give his or her best effort to help others achieve a goal. One's actions do indeed speak louder than words.

5	Evolve	Achieve increasingly better results	Results

Successful change produces desirable results from the start. Keeping focus on results is essential to achieving our goals. A process of evolution takes us upward on the ascent.

Once we set on a destination, the actual journey consists of small steps. The cumulative impact of consistent progress leads, in the end, to significant gains. Sustainable progress comes from evolution—a process of continuous improvements.

Measurement is at the core of continuous improvement. When a goal is measured, it becomes important. As the measures are reported, our attention focuses on improving results. The rate of measuring, reporting, and improving sets the pace of change. By systematically discovering and eliminating causes of errors, we can accelerate change.

Performance measures help people hold each other accountable for what they can control. We can influence change when we track performance measures that indicate how our actions impact results. As we learn from our mistakes or from errors inherent in a system, we can improve incrementally. Continuous learning helps us consistently achieve better results.

The Five Ascent Principles take us on an upward course, while overcoming the negative tendencies of the Roller Coaster Ride. Each of the five principles counters a corresponding widening gap described in the previous chapter. You can overcome distrust by creating a shared story of success that builds common purpose. You can reduce lack of focus by clarifying your team's direction through concrete objectives and a strategically agile plan. You can overcome low capability by deploying the right people into key roles and developing everyone's strengths. You can increase commitment by inspiring teamwork and collaboration. Results accelerate as you instill discipline for tracking performance measures. The following chart describes how the Five Ascent Principles close the five widening gaps.

Closing the Widening Gaps with The Ascent Principles

Low Trust	1	Create the story of success	Purpose
Lack of Focus	2	Seize the opportunity for change	Direction
Poor Capability	3	Develop capacity from strengths	Capacity
Weak Commitment	4	Inspire collaboration and teamwork	Commitment
Delayed Results	5	Achieve increasingly better results	Results

In the next five chapters we are going to explore how each of these principles were behind the success at each of the Change Masters and many other organizations, teams, and individuals.

In chapter four, we will learn how Apple was inspired by Steve Jobs to envision a line of highly successful products and services long before they existed or were even possible to make. Chapter five highlights the story of a monolithic IBM corporation quickly becoming focused on its customers' priorities as Lou Gerstner infused them with a powerful dose of reality. Chapter six describes how James McNerney overcame decades of stagnation at 3M and how Carlos Ghosn avoided Nissan's imminent bankruptcy by urgently deploying talented people and rapidly developing new capabilities. In chapter seven, we walk right into the job of saving Xerox, following Anne Mulcahy's bravely engaged employees' and customers' commitment under dismal conditions. Finally, in chapter nine we learn how to achieve consistently better results from Andy Grove's culture of discipline at Intel and Caterpillar's dedication to continuous improvement under James Owens's steady global expansion.

But before we dive deep into each Ascent Principle at the Change Masters, let's review how every person's example influences the ascent process. Far removed from the world of business, we learn from a group of mountaineers what it takes to successfully scale one of the most dangerous ascents of the Swiss Alps.

The Ascent of the Eiger

Rising straight upward from the pleasant meadows of the Swiss Alps, the north face of the Eiger represents for mountain climbers an extreme test of skill and character. Reaching the 13,000-foot summit by scaling the dark and forbidding north face has challenged mountaineers from around the world.

Early climbers described this savage precipice as inaccessible, and for most of the year, the Eiger's north face remains truly inaccessible. Shrouded in ice, swept by avalanches, and veiled by frequent storms, few had been able to scale past the bottom half of this wall.

Every climber who reaches the upper wall of the Eiger's north face has to go through the "white spider." There is no way around it. This eerily steep section has won its name for its likeness to a gigantic spider, with "legs" that extend hundreds of feet in every direction from the main body of ice, through cracks, gullies, and crevices. On the white spider, even the most skilled and swiftest of climbers meet the toughest test.

By the summer of 1938, nobody had yet been able to reach the summit. A record of casualties, near fatalities, and last-minute retreats had left a vivid imprint in the memory of Alpine mountaineers. This included the deaths of two young Italian climbers during an early season attempt on the Eiger's north face.

Despite the evident danger, on July 21, 1938, Fritz Vasparek and Heinrich Harrer started to go up the north face. Before dawn, they met with another party, Anderl Heckmair and Ludwig Vorg, two renowned Alpine climbers. A third team was also on its way up, but a falling rock injured one of them and halted their expedition.

A few hours into the climb, Vasparek and Harrer perched themselves on a narrow ledge for rest and breakfast. When they resumed their march, Heckmair and Vorg were already ahead of them. The two teams continued climbing as separate groups, often overtaking each other in a competitive spirit.

The more experienced climbers, Heckmair and Vorg, eventually took the lead. Heckmair in particular was a confident lead climber of unusual strength. He was able to climb holding the rope with one hand while using his other hand to carve steps with his ice axe. Heckmair's single-handed trailblazing talent kept the rest moving at a steady pace.

On the second day of the climb, the teams were to cross the infamous white spider. As the ascent became more strenuous, they decided to join on a single rope. Cooperating as a foursome, they scaled one of the legs of the spider, a 100-foot vertical crack, which provided the only possible line of ascent.

As they were making slow progress, a sudden storm enveloped the team in thick clouds, and they lost visibility of each other and the surrounding precipice. By the time the team managed to reach the main ice field that forms the body of the spider, it had begun to sleet and snow. Flashes of lighting and roaring thunder shook them, and the wind howled at them with fury.

Mixed with the whistling sounds of the storm, they heard the distinctive hiss of an avalanche. As soon as the climbers recognized the sound, they clung to whatever hold they had. Kasparek, who was in the lead position, instinctively drove a piton into the rock. A collapsing shower of rocks and ice fell on them, threatening to break their hold. None of the climbers knew whether their fellow climbers were still standing or sliding down with the avalanche.

As the pressure finally decreased, each climber noticed that the rope was still tight, indicating that at least one of their fellow climbers was still holding on. Before they could breathe a sigh of relief, however, another avalanche hit, even more intense than the first one. It was only to be expected at this point that the entire team would be wiped from the face of the mountain.

Just as the climbers' last reserves of strength and air were exhausted, the avalanches stopped. In the darkness, they began calling each other's names. Through the thick air they heard a response back. Every person in the team was still holding on. By holding firmly to the rope that united them, they had managed to live. They felt overjoyed, as if they have been saved by a miracle.

The piton that Kasparek had driven into the rock just as the first avalanche hit had kept all of them anchored to the rock. Realizing that the entire team depended on this piton staying firm, Kasparek had protected it with his body against falling rocks and ice. Although he received several hits and scratches, his will to protect the piton was greater. During the brief break between the two avalanches, Kasparek continued to drive the piton into the rock up to its ring and hooked himself to it just in time, saving the four-man line from falling into the abyss.

Heckmair and Vorg, the two men in the middle of the rope, didn't have a firm hold on the wall and were swept from their positions. The impact of their fall on the rope could have easily torn off the piton. Realizing they were sliding downhill, Heckmair drove his ice axe into the ice to form an anchor and with his other arm he held his partner from the collar the entire time. Vorg's life was saved by Heckmair's unyielding grip. A team effort kept the entire team alive.

The overwhelming joy of their survival was the triumph of self-sacrificing team spirit. At the point of everyone's last reserves, they drew strength from their character. As their initial competitiveness dissolved into a firm union that took them to the summit, they formed a bond of friendship that helped them conquer the mountain.[15]

In the summer of 1938, four individuals started up the Eiger, but one team reached the top. Leading an organization through change in unpredictable times is akin to the first successful ascent of the Eiger's north face. The principles and practices for overcoming challenging situations in order to reach daring goals are universal and timeless—no matter the situation. While our physical lives may not be as exposed as they would be on the north face of the Eiger, our mental and emotional capacities are tested to the extreme in times of change.

Figuratively, there are times when our life hangs from a rope, as if suspended in midair on the face of a dangerous cliff. In such situations we need something or someone on which we can depend. The carabiner anchored to the solid rock, holding our weight through a descending avalanche, stands as a symbol of the need for a reliable foundation based on principles. The rope suggests that there is someone else holding on to the other side of rope, facilitating our ascent.

The nature of change will follow its course heedless of our courage, determination, or ambition. External conditions may rage all around us, but our will to do our best for the benefit of others can be stronger than all the external conditions combined. The key to success is the choice we make at the point of expending our last reserves—our determination to follow the Path of Ascent.

> *The achievements of an organization*
> *are the results of the combined effort*
> *of each individual.*
>
> ~Vince Lombardi

## PART TWO

The Five Ascent Principles

The Ascent Process
5Es for Mastering Change

Build Common Purpose	Clarify Direction	Develop Capacity	Inspire Commitment	Achieve Results
Envision	Evaluate	Empower	Engage	Evolve
What do we want to see happen?	How can we make it happen?	How do we build on strengths?	How do we inspire collaboration?	How do we track progress?

## CHAPTER FOUR

Build Common Purpose
Envision: What do we want to see happen?

The future never just happened.
It was created.

~Will and Ariel Durant

Got Vision?

We all have a vision. It may be simple or grand, but that is not what makes the difference between ultimate success and failure. The decisive factor is the intent. The greatest difference is between a vision that is widely shared and deeply held, and one that is narrowly focused on one's self. Building common purpose is about creating a vision for the greater good. As we focus on others' needs and address broader interests, we overcome the negative influence of low trust. Most visions fail to inspire others simply because they are self centered. What kind of vision have you got?

This simple concept had kept a little known New Mexico factory breaking records for over 10 years. Their vision of building a high performing work environment meant more to them than a mere job. Their deeply held and widely shared vision of success had grown into a mighty purpose binding them together for over a decade of outstanding success.

"They requested your services, so they are the ones who will interview you," the plant manager informed me as he introduced me to a group of factory workers, called Cereal Manufacturing Technicians, or CMTs for short. I had been asked to help improve leadership skills at one of General Mills' top performing plants, so I had assumed—until that moment—that I would be working with the plant management. Clad in white uniforms, the CMTs bombarded me with questions to determine if I was the kind of consultant they wanted to hire.

My puzzled look at the decision latitude and broad responsibilities of the CMTs must have been obvious to them. "You are not used to this," one said, attempting to clue me in. "We are a high performance culture," he added proudly. I had heard about the concept, but I had never before experienced it.

Over the ensuing three years I had the opportunity to work alongside the CMTs at this plant. In the process, I learned a lot about what it means to work in a high performance environment. At this plant, CMTs literally ran the entire operation. They decided whom to hire or fire and who got paid what. They also decided how much and what types of cereal to make, and how to run their schedules. They conducted experiments to improve quality, productivity, and innovation. They did all this with minimal direction from management.

"So what do you do?" I asked the plant manager one day. He responded, "Our job is to facilitate production. We analyze information and propose ways to improve the system. We are constantly learning about best practices and sharing them with the CMTs." Then he paused and leaned forward in his chair, as if he were about to disclose the best kept secret. "Our main job," he said, almost whispering, "is to keep the philosophy alive and vibrant."

Maintaining a philosophy is hardly how a typical plant manager would describe his main responsibility. When I quizzed him on what he actually did to keep the philosophy alive and vibrant, he said, "We make sure we live it!" He went on to tell me how 10 years earlier, the plant was started with a vision.

In the early days of operation, workers and managers met often to envision the most productive working environment imaginable.

They learned the principles of high performance. They aligned all decisions with the goal of achieving the highest quality and productivity possible at the lowest cost. In their envisioned state, the plant was to be run not by the management hierarchy, but by centers of competency, made up mostly of CMTs. Workers would be making significant decisions, often consulting with other workers within their team. Managers were to act as performance coaches, making recommendations for system improvements. Few power plays would exist because performance, rather than position, would be the primary source of power.

At one point a progressive CMT left the plant, attracted by higher wages at the Intel plant across the street. Within nine months he was back. When questioned about his decisions, he simply explained that after learning the high performance philosophy, he did not want to go back to working under strict supervision. "I didn't have any problems with my supervisor," he explained. "I just had no need for a boss telling me what to do."

By the time of my visit, the vision had been kept alive and vibrant for a full 10 years. Their high performance hinged on maintaining that vision. For each of the 10 years, this plant had set performance records for the entire company in productivity, quality, innovation, safety, and profitability. As every employee faithfully learned and willingly embraced the high performance philosophy, the business and the employees thrived.

The consulting experience at General Mills left a distinctive mark in my memory. A few years after my three-year involvement at that plant, I was asked to return. I arrived at the plant with great anticipation, but I soon realized that things had changed. An entirely new management team had taken over the plant. Many of the old CMTs had left, and the plant was no longer first in five of the seven key performance measures.

The current group of managers wanted to know what they could do to get it back on track. When I explained to them the high performance philosophy, they quickly brushed it aside. They did not want to talk about vision. They wanted tangible things—processes, programs, and policies—they could use to manage performance. I realized then that the vision had been lost.

Before leaving, I made a quick visit to the manufacturing floor, hoping to find some of the former CMTs. I recognized a few, and I went up to one of them and asked him what had happened to the original philosophy. I expected him to talk openly, as he had before, and take initiative to tackle any problem. Instead, he looked at me as if I was from another planet. He simply told me he had to stay on task and that I would get in trouble for being there. "In trouble with whom?" I asked lightly, assuming he was kidding me. He replied, dead serious, "In trouble with the boss."

On my way to the airport I wondered what had happened. How could a culture that had been so alive and vibrant be lost so quickly? Why had the new managers failed to embrace the philosophy that had given that plant 10 years of record performance? Why had the CMTs who had experienced such high levels of engagement, openness, and trust abandoned the vision that made work worth more than its mere pay? The answer was simply that they had lost their original purpose.

> # Living the vision
> # keeps it alive and vibrant.

The new management introduced a less inspiring purpose. Their desire was simply to run the operation. The ideal of being the best place to work or the most productive place quickly flew out the window. Some workers, unable to reconcile themselves to the new philosophy, left the company. Those who stayed lowered standards and adjusted to the all-too-familiar rules of management until they fully accepted them. It soon became "just a job."

The only way to keep a vision alive and vibrant is to live it every day. You have to work at it, sacrifice for it, and persistently pursue it as if the dream is all that really matters to you. Otherwise, the vision soon becomes a lofty ideal, a venerable statement on a wall that is impractical and rare in everyday interactions. Let's explore how an ordinary group of people, working an average job, can actually live up to their vision on a daily basis.

Dreams are extremely important.
You can't do it unless you can imagine it.

~George Lucas

Finding a Powerful Purpose

We all want to be part of something greater than ourselves. We want to find purpose in our everyday experience—something that can give meaning to our lives. Unfortunately, few people ever find that higher meaning and fulfilling purpose in their work.

Some see their jobs as monotonous, routine, and rather boring. They wished they could be doing something far more interesting. Others find themselves limited by the circumstances, mired in rules, policies, and regulations that stifle initiative. They wish they could be working in a more progressive department or dynamic organization. A third group feels utterly confined by a supervisor who controls their every thought and move. This group usually wishes for a position of authority so they can call the shots and be free to act for themselves.

As long as we are resigned to feeling trapped, we are doomed to spend a large part of our life simply serving time in the name of a higher purpose somewhere else outside of work. This doesn't need to be the case! We can change our situation by simply finding a powerful purpose in what we do at work.

A powerful purpose is born out of a genuine desire to become the best at doing what brings the most value to us and others. Making the world better does not need to be a monumental act. Much good is accomplished daily in a small ways.

Within our immediate circle of influence, we can find numerous opportunities to find greater meaning in our work. Establishing trust with a coworker, facilitating more open communications between peers, and doing our very best work are all fulfilling purposes. As a team, we can become more cohesive, more responsive to each other, and more reliable at meeting deadlines. As we look beyond our immediate work group, we can establish better communications with other departments and functions by sharing information more openly and gaining a better understanding of what they do.

As an organization, building a better product, delivering a faster service, or making something more affordable can be truly inspiring purposes. We can find a powerful purpose in doing what brings the most value to a larger group of people—all the employees, every customer, and even the local communities the organization serves. In turn, investors will receive a sustainable return.

> # A powerful purpose is to become best at doing what brings the most value to us and others.

How can others perceive your purpose? We judge ourselves by our intentions, which we tend to fully justify, but which are wholly invisible to others. Others, on the other hand, judge us by our words and actions. What others perceive is the only valid information they have to form their opinion. The question we must often ask ourselves is: What motives do we communicate by our words and actions?

Terry had assembled a strong group of "A" players to lead his up-and-coming technology firm. They represented the industry's top picks, all bearing impressive credentials and bringing along a proven track record of success. Each had left behind promising positions and joined the newly formed team, at a great expense to the company.

As expected of top performers, they were highly competitive. Interpersonal differences soon escalated into trust issues that affected their entire functions. In a few months, the promising team was failing, and taking down the entire company with them.

Terry called for an emergency meeting for team members to put their differences behind and get onboard. This resulted in a series of public accusations that widened the gap between them. "How do we get this group to work together as a team?" Terry asked me in distress. The process, I said, would require open conversation, not about their differences, but about what they have in common. We needed to discover their common purpose.

A second all-day meeting was scheduled soon after the first one. This time, the focus was on building common ground by clarifying the group's mission, vision, and values. Particular attention was paid to describing what actions supported or contradicted the organization's values. Most leaders soon found ways to collaborate with each other by making personal adjustments. One decided to leave the company and one was asked to resign. The remaining group formed a powerful team that successfully took the company forward.

If we want to increase trust, we start by building a common purpose. Creating the story of success begins by finding what objectives team members have in common. Building on common ground, the team can identify shared values by discussing actions that support or contradict their aspirations. When a team's actions are consistent with their values, trust increases. Further confidence comes by describing what success looks like. A vivid description of desired outcomes binds a team to a common purpose.

Building Common Purpose

MUTUAL PURPOSE
Find objectives all team members
have in common.

SHARED VALUES
Discuss the behaviors that
support (or contradict) team values.

DESIRED OUTCOMES
Describe what success looks like.

Leading a team with a powerful purpose requires inspiring others to see exciting opportunities in the current condition. Inspiring leaders find ways to reframe potentially discouraging situations into uplifting ones. This does not mean that a visionary leader is unrealistic or sees the world through rose-colored glasses. Quite the opposite, the most inspiring leaders are firmly grounded in reality while maintaining an unyielding faith in the future.

A deeply held and widely shared vision transcends reality. Some say that faith can move mountains. Vision has the power to move people, even large organizations, to do great things. Even seemingly impossible goals are achieved every day by the power of vision.

So many of our dreams seem impossible,
then improbable, then inevitable.

~Christopher Reeve

Creating the Story of Success

Ever since humans gathered in a circle around a fire, storytelling has been the means to share important ideas and pass on valuable traditions. Good storytelling captivates people with the vision of what is meaningful and possible.

It is possible for a single person to have a grand vision. But turning that vision into reality requires that many other people adopt that vision and work in concert to achieve it. Envisioning desired outcomes helps us achieve what we want to become.

The best way to create the future is to first describe it and then work diligently to help make it happen. The creative power of envisioning results in a story of our future success that describes what we want to become. We start with random thoughts of what that future looks like. As we combine these thoughts into ideas, we start weaving a story. Sharing the story allows us to communicate, refine, and influence our actions.

Stories can propel us forward to reach our full potential or limit us within our own mental prison. The stories we construct about ourselves—and about others—shape most aspects of our lives. The stories we believe in define what we think is possible, what opportunities we think we have, and what goals we believe we can achieve.

An entrepreneur friend of mine invited me to participate in envisioning, with the help of others, the concept for a new business. She invited people from diverse backgrounds for two days of intense envisioning. Representing various cultural and professional backgrounds, this group of people brought along innovative business ideas and, more importantly, a keen sense of curiosity, to help create a specialty tea business that blends exotic tea leaves with social tea time.

While sipping tea flavors from around the world, they imagined the in-store experience from every angle—from the distinctive red lamp outside the store entrance to the smell of tea leaves welcoming the incoming guests. Their common purpose was to help create an experience powerful enough to develop a taste for tea in people of all ages and cultures.

In a couple of days, group members shared their personal ideas, crafted a compelling storyline for the promising new venture, and participated in animated storytelling contests. In the process, they helped form an exciting concept for the new enterprise concept. After additional weeks of story crafting and editing, an illustrated narrative emerged that described in vivid detail the compelling story of the envisioned enterprise. The appeal of the concept sold investors and helped raise the capital needed to launch the venture.

Envisioning the end is enough
to put the means in motion.

~Dorothea Brande

Creating a new business concept is no different from designing a new product, enhancing an existing service, or improving one's life. As new ideas are spoken, shaped, and revised, they evolve into a compelling story. The power of the story can then help turn ideas into future realities.

Many business strategies jump right into analytical problem solving, entirely skipping the creative visioning step. Without visionary exploration, decisions often fall into rote solutions to standard needs. Strategies that start with creative envisioning discover innovative answers with ingenious approaches.

As you move through the creative envisioning process, collaboration helps overcome personal creative limitations and cognitive blind spots. The recipe for breakthrough innovation consists of abundant amounts of collaboration, open dialogue, hard work, and feedback for every measure of creative genius.

*Genius is one percent inspiration and
ninety-nine percent perspiration.*

~Thomas A. Edison

A more insidious barrier to success comes from limiting ourselves. I know some people who are unhappy with the way their life is turning out. They feel as if they have become victims trapped in a plot from which they cannot escape. They are no longer the actors but the spectators of their lives.

Once, after a training session, I met with a woman who shared with me her terribly sad story of abuse, divorce, sickness, and isolation. Then she said to me that it was as if she was sitting in a movie cinema watching the story of her life play out on the large screen. "As I watched it," she said to me, "I thought to myself: I just don't like this movie!" However, she said she kept watching it, hoping that somehow, someone would make it better. As the movie went on she realized it was getting worse. Finally, she was so disgusted with the film, that she turned to a person who was sitting next to her, and said, "I hate this movie! I can't stand it. It's an awful story. I'm not even sure why I'm here still watching it."

Then, the person turned to her and, with a surprised expression, he simply said, "This is *your* movie. *You* are making it this way. Why don't we just walk to another room and watch a better movie?" With tears in her eyes, she looked at me and said, "It was that simple. Five years ago, I decided to create a different story for my life—one I would really like, and one that others would enjoy watching with me as well. For most of my life, I kept blaming others for my life, when all along I was the one writing the script."

We should not let our fears hold us
back from pursuing our hopes.

~John F. Kennedy

We can take ownership for our life story as we realize that, for the most part, we write the script. It's true that life doesn't always go as planned. We all face situations beyond our control. We will experience setback and disappointments, but we are still writing the script.

These events, if we let them, can devastate us, leaving us victims of situations beyond our control. However, these situations can also become unexpected twists that make our lives richer and more interesting. As we pick up the plot where it now stands, we can write the story of our future success.

We can overcome mental barriers and inspire substantial growth by setting a positive challenge. We enlist others commitment to a vision by sharing with them bold and worthwhile goals. These aren't just stretch goals; they are not even very ambitious goals. These are goals that challenge us beyond our comfort zone, to the point where we have to take a leap of faith into the dark. If we believe we can do it, we jump!

In May 1961, John F. Kennedy gave a speech before a concerned Congress to address the state of the Cold War. In many ways, the United States had been falling behind the Soviet Union. He ended his speech by unexpectedly challenging the nation with a goal: "I believe that this nation should commit itself to achieving the goal, before this decade is out, of landing a man on the moon and returning him safely to the earth. . . . If we make this judgment in the affirmative, it will not be one man going to the moon, it will be an entire nation. For all of us must work to put him there."

Sending a man to the moon had been beyond anything anyone had ever done at that time. Committing to this vision created a rallying point for the entire nation. Within eight years man walked on the moon, and the unifying vision took the United States closer to fulfilling its leadership mission.

A goal is a dream with a deadline.

~Diana Scharf Hunt

Companies make great steps forward by setting visionary goals. In the early 1980s, Microsoft set the goal of "a personal computer in every home, running Microsoft software." At the time, that goal would have been considered highly unrealistic, even nearly impossible. Yet many were inspired to achieve such a visionary goal. In a few decades, this objective has been essentially accomplished. Companies daring to dream big often achieve great things.

Creating the story of success may take several iterations. We may need to enlist the help of others. It may require us to revise our own script and remove our limiting barriers. We may have to go beyond our comfort zone and leap into the unknown. What we have in the end is the power to shape the future.

There are those who look at things the way they are, and ask why . . . I dream of things that never were, and ask why not?

~Robert F. Kennedy

Envisioning the Future

Among the Change Masters, the story of Apple and Steve Jobs best illustrates the transforming power of vision. Apple's success as a technology innovator reveals how winning products originate by thinking of the user and seeing possibilities ahead of any articulated customer need. Steve Jobs was constantly observing how people use products, watching consumer trends, and thinking of ways to improve on what others were already doing. He was constantly envisioning the future.

One day in 1983 Steve Jobs walked into a meeting at Apple headquarters carrying a conspicuous plastic bag. He turned it upside down, and placed onto the conference table a flat object that looked like a beige desk diary. All eyes were fixed on the strange object. Surely this was one of Steve's latest ideas, but no one was sure exactly what it was.

At that time, Jobs was head of the Apple Computers division that was producing the Macintosh computer. At his request a pirate flag flew above the building, representing the renegade spirit of the Mac enterprise. He welcomed ideas no matter where they came from, especially if the ideas were founded on successful products unrelated to computers. Jobs enjoyed placing all sorts of product prototypes in front of employees to watch them play with the objects and collect their feedback.

Employees at that meeting must have suspected this was just another prototype for their feedback—maybe a portable keyboard or a hard drive. Jobs opened the object, and the onlookers saw something totally unexpected. There were hinges along one of the edges, and it opened like a book. One half was a mock-up keyboard. "The other was a computer monitor, like a small TV screen. But *flat*."[16]

"This is my dream of what we'll be making in the mid to late 80s," Jobs told his bemused colleagues. "We won't reach this on Mac One or Mac Two, but it will be Mac Three. This will be the culmination of all this Mac stuff."[17]

With help from leading designers, Jobs showed us the future— a portable computer! "Even though Steve didn't draw any of the lines, his ideas and inspiration taught us how to design today's laptop. 'We didn't know what it meant for a computer to be "friendly" until Steve told us.'"[18]

Eight years later, in 1991, Apple introduced the PowerBook, a revolutionary notebook PC that weighed about five pounds. It wasn't the first laptop on the market, but it was clearly the best. Almost overnight, it became the best-selling computer in the United States, with $1 billion in sales in its first year.

But the success didn't last. In January 1996, Apple Computers was losing money and market share; the besieged company cut 1,300 jobs. Michael Spindler, Apple's president and chief executive officer, said, "The most immediate and obvious work we must undertake is to quickly streamline operations. The work-force reduction is a necessary first step." Apple observers weren't impressed with the announcement. "I see no new strategy. I see sort of a Band-Aid to stop the hemorrhaging, and not a very effective Band-Aid at that," reported Pieter Hartsook, publisher of the *Hartsook Letter*.[19]

A year later, despite efforts to restructure, reorganize, and streamline operations, Apple executives proved unable to steer the company out of trouble. Apple kept losing market share, laying off workers, and rotating CEOs, all while turning off potential buyers. The company was running out of time. When Steve Jobs officially took over as CEO of Apple in 1997, the company was just about out of business.

Jobs immediately helped raise the struggling company's sights, beginning one of the most successful turnaround stories on the Path of Ascent. Rather than bashing his predecessors or focusing on solving Apple's escalating crises, Jobs instead pitched his vision for innovative products. He turned the company focus back on the customers rather than on its competitors. In fact, Jobs went so far as partnering with Apple's long-time nemesis, Microsoft, a move that instantly removed doubts over Apple's survival and opened its products to the entire market.

Jobs revamped Apple's distribution system and operations, and leveraged its most valuable asset—its brand. He called for a platform that could seamlessly merge computing, media, telecommunications, and mobile Internet services. The introduction of the iMac marked the start of a string of "i" products that embraced a new vision for the mobile Internet age. The hallmark change came in 2001, with the introduction of the iPod, followed by the iTunes service, and later the iPhone.

By describing a vision of the future, Jobs inspired industrial designers, software engineers, and other industry players to launch a wave of highly innovative products. Jobs' vision reinvented an existing product category by turning cell phones into stylish music boxes and pocket computers. In the process, Jobs reinvented Apple to become, once again, the innovation leader in technology, taking the share price from $4 in 1997 to $100 in 2007.[20]

The most effective leader is one who sees and
harnesses the transforming power of vision.

~Beth Davis

Envisioning is the art of storytelling. We all have stories to tell. People and organizations succeed or fail by their ability to tell their story. In the process, we reveal motives, convey a vision, and communicate values. Have you ever paused to ponder what makes up the story of your life? The story of your family? The story of your work group?

To begin writing the story of your future success, describe what it would be like to have achieved a desired result. Talk about it in present tense, as if had already happened. Pick a specific point in time and state what meaningful change has been achieved by reaching the milestone. Express in as much detail as possible the thinking, attitudes, and behaviors then present. Let the narrative capture the moment with vivid emotion and precise facts. The more real and compelling, the more powerful the story will become as a guiding force into the envisioned future.

As you share this story with others, it becomes more meaningful. If the story inspires you as well as others, it builds momentum for action. As actions lead people forward toward the envisioned future, the story becomes credible. The story makes the task worth pursuing, binding people to act in unison. The power of purpose holds people together through the test of time.

> # The power of purpose holds people together through the test of time.

Leaders motivate people to action through compelling stories. Success stories, well told, engage people's imagination and commitment. Stories of heroes and heroines teach us what is possible and desirable. Stories about the future tell us about products and services we can design and build. Behind any great endeavor there is a compelling story that propels people forward.

Unfortunately, most companies' vision statements do not function as compelling or effective stories. The vast majority of corporate vision statements end up placed on a web site or a noticeable wall, and are quickly forgotten by the people who work there, revisited only once in a while during management retreats or in corporate reports to the shareholders.

In contrast, a vibrant and living vision exists in the stories that people tell to their peers. These stories spread as they are told and retold in people's own words. They remain relevant as they explain why we do what we do.

This is the reason why the vision behind the continuing success at the cereal manufacturing plant was suddenly lost. The vision was abandoned. The purpose changed. The new management introduced a different, more mundane story. The workers stopped passing on the former stories that filled them with a sense of purpose.

The vision was still there as an ideal, but not as a living philosophy guiding daily choices. Slowly, the CMTs forgot those stories as more rational themes took over. Some began to question if some of the stories were even accurate. Certainly, they did not seem practical any longer. In only a few years, the philosophy was abandoned as the stories became no more than historical tales.

Imagination is more powerful than knowledge.

~Albert Einstein

We can reclaim the vision of our enterprise by telling stories of success to each other. People are energized when they hear compelling stories about where they came from, why they do what they are doing, and where they are headed. The spark of everyday heroism inspires others to do likewise and be part of something great.

As people hear stories of success, they too become inspired and pledge their support to generate more success. The power of success stories attracts successful people—talented employees and loyal customers. They in turn become storytellers, passing the great news on to others. As we tell our story by word and action, soon the vision of our enterprise is alive and vibrant once again. The vision needs to be imbedded in the culture in order to become and remain a driving force.

Every battle is won before it is ever fought.

~Sun Tzu

Discovering Our Success Stories

Envisioning the future has played an important role in my life. Perhaps my most intense envisioning experience occurred when I was 25 years old. I had been married for only about two years, we had just had our first son, and I was starting my first big job. I was working for the IBM Corporation at the world headquarters in the Armonk, New York, Management Development Center. By most measures, my life was going great, but in some ways, I was feeling completely lost.

I had no idea what I wanted to do to earn a living. I was working in my field of study and for one of the best organizations. I was doing reasonably well and putting in long hours. I was earning very good money, too. But I could not see myself spending my life in a corporate career. Those closest to me could tell that deep inside, I was struggling.

Every evening, by the time I arrived at our studio apartment in Danbury, Connecticut, after an hour and a half commute, I would lay on the floor exhausted. I tried to listen to my wife, who had been alone with our infant son the entire day. Since we had only one car, she had been waiting for my arrival so we could shop for groceries. She also expected some non-baby talk before I fell asleep. For almost nine months, the same routine went on uninterrupted. I was becoming a casualty of my own career choice. I needed to know what I wanted to do with my life, which was certainly not what I was doing then!

On a sunny Saturday morning in early autumn, I went to the woods near Lake Candlewood with a pen, a pad of paper, and a prayer in my heart. I wanted—I *needed*—to know what to do with my life. I realized that no one would tell me what to do. I needed to figure it out myself and go for it.

After contemplating the inspiring New England fall scene, I drew a straight line on the paper pad and wrote numbers representing years from the present extending 12 years into the future. In my mind I went to the year 2003 and pictured myself leading a consulting firm and working with a team of about a dozen people with clients all over the world. I pictured a home right by the mountains and four children running around the neighborhood. I saw myself serving in my community among other immigrants, mostly Hispanic.

Before the image faded from my mind, I scribbled on the pad of paper key words and phrases about that envisioned day 12 years into the future. Then, I went back, placing dots along the timeline that marked events leading up to the envisioned state. I anticipated each of the children's births and our ages. I set a time for the purchase of our first house, and later on moving to another one in the mountains. I set a goal 5 years from that day for launching the consulting business.

I have kept that timeline. It has proven to be surprisingly accurate for my life—not that I planned my life by it, but it has given me a sense of direction that allowed me to fulfill my purpose. In addition, the vision also helped me carry out my work at IBM much better.

I have gained so much from that experience that since then I have kept the habit of taking time every fall to envision my work and my life. Some year's visions have been predictable extensions of the previous year's directions. In such cases I have been able to update my goals and restate my ideals in a single page. Other years have been critical transition points, filled with personal growth and learning. On such occasions, I have written multiple pages packed with new insights, ambitious goals, and vivid descriptions of the future.

The envisioning process has helped me choose my path, anticipate transitions, and prepare for what was ahead. I have come to realize that envisioning blends a degree of personal revelation and some creative inspiration with a heavy dose of perspiration. Deciding what we want for our work and our life requires that we exercise faith in the future, take creative license, and apply ourselves to diligent labor.

Envisioning has helped many organizations clarify their mission, their aspirations, and their future state. In doing so, they have been able to describe with confidence their mission, their values, and the story of their success. In the process, they clarify the type of workers they want to attract and the skills they want to develop. In some cases, they even describe products and services or markets and customers not yet in existence, but that are effectively foreseen. Envisioning is the power to create the future.

As you dream, so shall you become. Your vision
is the promise of what you shall at last unveil.

~John Ruskin

Chapter Review

Summary

Vision inspires people to do great things through the power of purpose. In order to have a vibrant vision, we need to live it every day. If we don't feel people are inspired by a vision at work, we need to discover a powerful purpose. Individuals can find purpose in becoming better at doing what brings the most value to themselves and others. A leader can help a team discover a powerful purpose by helping team members clarify the mission, vision, and values of the team. The vision becomes influential as it describes the story of the team's future success.

Key Points

- We build trust by finding a common purpose.
- Defining a group's mission, vision, and values helps create a common purpose.
- The following steps build trust through a common purpose:
  1. Clarify the team's primary purpose.
  2. Describe the team's story of success.
  3. Discuss what actions support or contradict the team values.

Group Discussion

1. To what extent do we feel inspired by a vibrant vision at work?
2. What is our team's primary purpose?
3. What is our team's story of future success?
4. What everyday actions support or contradict our values?
5. How can we make the story of success more credible?

Access additional Ascent Tools at
www.ascent-advisor.com/tools.html

The Ascent Process
5Es for Mastering Change

Build Common Purpose	Clarify Direction	Develop Capacity	Inspire Commitment	Achieve Results
Envision	Evaluate	Empower	Engage	Evolve
What do we want to see happen?	How can we make it happen?	How do we build on strengths?	How do we inspire collaboration?	How do we track progress?

## CHAPTER FIVE

Clarify Direction
Evaluate: How can we make it happen?

Vision without action is merely a dream.
Action without vision merely passes the time.
Vision with action can change the world.

~Joel Barker

Adapting to Changing Conditions

Envision, the first step on the Path of Ascent, helps us visualize the desired outcome. The next step, Evaluate, is about planning a course of action to take us forward. While envisioning is conceptual and future-oriented, evaluation is concrete and realistic. There is nothing particularly new about creating an action plan to meet one's goals. The key, however, is being able to adjust plans with changing conditions, while staying focused on the strategic objectives. The ability to evaluate conditions in real time is what gave Kevin and his team the edge when others foundered.

"We want to get closer to our customers," said Kevin to his executive team. That was a scary thought as none of them had ever seen the customer nor sold their fruit directly. The risks of breaking away from the established distribution model posed real threats. But the opportunities created by selling directly to the customer were very attractive, and Kevin concluded that they could do better on their own.

Traditionally, fruit is sold through a cooperative representing a conglomerate of large and small growers. The distribution system has been around for decades. The decision for one of them to sell their fruit directly was a radical industry change.

Kevin gathered his executive team to discuss the implications of the new strategy and to plan for flawless execution. The company would have to establish relationships with customers they had never met. They would have to win the customers' trust in their ability to deliver fruit according to exact requirements. They would have to learn to market and sell the product with the agility of seasoned experts from day one. Moreover, they would have to embrace an entire sales function and mindset.

At the strategic planning meeting, Kevin and his team discussed the implications of making this move, identifying specific objectives and milestones. They reviewed the profile of the sales team that would have to come onboard. A deciding factor in the selection of sales people was their proven ability to sell high volumes of fruit, as the company was a major supplier.

Having the right people onboard was just the first step. Then, they would have to get everyone up to speed and integrated into the organization. They would have to understand the entire production process from beginning to end. They would have to deploy and learn to use a new system. All of this would need to happen in just a few months, before the season started.

Kevin and his team carefully planned every aspect of the launch and executed it with precision. After the launch, everything was working as planned. The sales team was off to a strong start and fully anticipating large volumes. Then, the unexpected happened.

Only three months after the sales force launch, a record-setting freeze threatened the company's entire inventory. Night after night for two full weeks the temperature dropped to freezing conditions, placing relentless strain on the fruits and the growers.

For the sales team, this meant not knowing what they had available to sell or if they would even have any fruit to sell at all. A full year's work could be gone in a single night. Since the inventory was at risk, Kevin decided to keep the entire staff working, doing what they could to evaluate the damage and protect the fruit to the greatest extent possible.

For the farming group, this meant working days and nights, often up to 20 hours a day, not knowing for how long. During the days, the experienced farming team assessed the inventory, salvaging every little lot of good fruit available. They also flooded as many fields as possible with water, because water radiates at night the heat collected during the day. When water freezes, it also releases energy.

In addition to flooding the fields, the farming team ran wind machines during the nights to push the warmer air trapped in the night-time atmosphere down through the trees. Trucks carrying large fuel tanks and the wind machines were positioned at different locations, and moved throughout the night to protect as many ranches as possible.

Everybody continued to work day after day, red-eyed and deeply tired, but without complaining. This was not their first weather event, but certainly it was the most intense and prolonged case in 100 years. Every day they would evaluate the condition of the fields and adjust resources for the night. Day after day, the same routine: assessment, feedback, planning, and execution helped them make the most of the unprecedented weather conditions.

At the packing plant, production experts adjusted the sorting equipment to accurately evaluate the condition of the fruit. Much of the fruit was saved and still good for the fresh market. Some fruit was sold for making juice.

The sales team evaluated the market conditions and decided to shift from a volume to a price strategy. Because the supply of fresh fruit was way down, prices went up temporarily, and the sales team decided to capitalize on the opportunity. While other growers were unable to supply their customers' needs, this company quickly moved in to fill the void.

Through constant assessment, feedback, and planning, they were able to make the best from the adverse situation. In fact, they came out of the freeze a stronger competitor in the fruit industry. "We had a good plan going into the year; we had planned for everything we could control," said Kevin, "but more importantly, we had a well-trained team of people able to respond to change and perform at their best when the situation became critical." The company performed at its peak despite unpredictable weather conditions in the critical year they launched their strategic change.

The brave heart that understands and
seizes the opportunity can do everything.

~Goethe

Seizing the Opportunities

Leading—or even functioning effectively—in uncertain and shifting conditions requires strategic agility. In the midst of ambiguity, strategic agility allows people to act decisively. It provides the guidance for making wise decisions when the future looks turbulent. So how can a team become strategically agile? It starts with having a clear understanding of the objectives and the role each person plays in carrying out the plan. More than relying on a rigid plan, however, strategic agility requires constant assessment and feedback. Planning and execution happen simultaneously and feed on each other.

Consider the strategic advantage of a special operations military unit dealing with fast-paced and high-risk conditions. The United States Navy Sea, Air, and Land Forces, commonly known as the Navy SEALs, for example, are employed in operations requiring decisive action. As a group, Navy SEALs are distinguished as individually reliable, collectively disciplined, and highly skilled. While other military forces are trained to follow strict orders, SEALs are conditioned to following their instincts in completing a mission. In such situations, success favors those able to respond quickly and intelligently.

No longer do bigger companies have the advantage over smaller ones. But we cannot conclude that smaller organizations are necessarily more agile. It is the ability to seize opportunities that gives any group of people the edge. This requires that people know how to create, capture, and sustain value in turbulent market conditions.

Agility calls for absolute clarity and focus coupled with freedom to act. With a thorough understanding of what an organization is trying to do, people are better able to make intelligent decisions and act responsibly. A strategically agile team sorts through competing demands and prioritizes multiple directions into effective action.

Teams, departments, and functions aiming to become more effective will benefit from clarifying their own strategy in relation to the overall organization. The process is essentially the same regardless of the size of the group. The steps include identifying concrete objectives, sizing up the scope, defining the group's unique value, and planning the course going forward. The framework below describes the components for achieving strategic agility.

Achieving Strategic Clarity

OBJECTIVE
Define concrete objectives for the team

SCOPE
Describe how, where, and when
the team will achieve the objectives

ADVANTAGE
Clarify the team's distinctive value
form the customer's perspective

PLAN
Discuss everyone's role
in making the plan successful

> **Strategic agility means
> that everyone understands
> the role they play in making
> the game plan successful.**

Can employees in your organization say what your strategy is? Most would avoid the question entirely. Some would attempt to answer with a general statement about the vision or mission of the organization—something like, "We are the best producer of this type of gadgets," or "We are the lowest cost provider of such and such service." Such answers aim at the company's mission and vision, but not at the strategy.

If you press further, the typical response is to jump right into the financial goals: revenue projections, sales quotas, or budget goals. People would say, "Our goal is to make so much revenue this year," or "We are going to increase profitability by so much before the next quarter."

The question remains: What is your organization's strategy? As the leader of your team, you can break this question into simpler ones: What are the group's objectives? How, where, and when are we going to achieve them? What unique value does our group contribute? and, Who is responsible for doing what? Strategic agility is achieved when everyone in the organization knows their part of the game plan and how to execute it.

Strategic agility is about seizing opportunities in the midst of rapid-fire change. In practical terms, this means that we must not strive for complete certainty before we act; in so doing we will cripple the initiative and pass up opportunities. Since decisions must be made in the face of uncertainty, there is no perfect solution to every situation.

Understanding the strategic objectives of the organization is the first step in helping employees become agile decision makers. People at all levels need to understand the organization's goals, not just by reciting the objectives and priorities, but by being able to explain the reasons behind those goals. Then they can anticipate and initiate changes in the approach while staying focused on the ultimate goals.

Clarity affords focus.

~Thomas Leonard

Setting Clear Objectives

Clear objectives are the first and most critical component of a company's strategy. A strategic objective is a precise goal that drives the business for the next three to five years. Most companies have revenue targets forecasting the future, but objectives are more than mere financial projections. A strategic objective provides a clear and compelling focus for the entire organization. A strategic objective is a concrete and motivating statement that is easy to grasp and remember.

Some have argued that during turbulent times, it is impossible to have clear objectives. In fact, it is in times of change when the need for clear objectives increases. If our goal has become a moving target, it doesn't mean that we no longer have a target. All it means is that we need a dynamic approach for aiming at it.

As businesses compete in increasingly crowded and volatile markets, those that have a clear focus are better able to stand out. Customers reward brands that convey a clear and consistent message. Defining a unique value to customers becomes even more important, since differentiated products and services command a premium, while less defined value propositions easily become commodities.

Strategic focus stands out as a key trait of the Change Masters. The companies that changed successfully were able to communicate a clear and consistent message about their direction and intended market position. Despite unpredictable conditions, their course was laser sharp.

The Strategic Objectives chart on the next page describes the business focus for each Change Master company in a single unambiguous statement. The direction of change was clear despite turbulent conditions in the industry. The message was consistently

Strategic Objectives
of the Change Masters

#	Company	Period	Business Focus
1	Intel	1994–1999	Transform from a manufacturer of memory chips into the world's leader of microprocessors.
2	Apple	2001–2005	Focus on meeting immediate customer needs by launching innovative products and services for the Internet age.
3	General Electric	1995–1999	Become the undisputed market leader in chosen industries by focusing on results.
6	IBM	1995–1999	Change the culture by focusing on customers and becoming the leader of high-end technology systems and services.
4	Caterpillar	2003–2006	Continue to build on the company's strengths through entrepreneurial global expansion.
5	McDonald's	2003–2006	Reinvent the brand as a health conscious and socially responsible company.
7	VeriSign	2003–2006	Introduce breakthrough innovations to mobile communications, commerce, and content services.
8	Nissan	2000–2004	Streamline operational costs, increase quality, and revitalize the product line through innovative cars.
9	3M	2000–2004	Improve quality, productivity, and focus on competitive products.
10	Xerox	2001–2005	Restore stakeholder confidence and reinvent the company as an innovator in smart document technology.

communicated to the customers. The market responded favorably to such clarity.

Conversely, the Change Failures seemed to be lost in a sea of initiatives, priorities, and mandates. Everyone was running like mad, but not much was really accomplished. The news articles covering what was happening at these companies often used words such as *unclear, erratic, vague, conflicting,* and *uncertain* in describing their direction.

Put this concept to a simple test. Ask the members of a leadership team to state their company's strategy and you are likely to come up with multiple answers. Not that the answers will be necessarily incorrect, but they will likely reflect varying levels of understanding and emphasis. If the leaders find it difficult to state the company's strategy, what hope is left for the rest of the managers and employees?

Clarifying the strategy is likely to ignite intense conversation among leaders as personal interpretations of the company's mission and vision are tried and tested under the pressure of specifics. In one case, partners at a financial investment firm confidently entered a discussion of their objectives, assuming their strategic alignment was evident. They were asked to describe their company's strategy. As they shared their personal views, a passionate debate ensued. A clear lack of strategic alignment became obvious, revealing a more insidious dysfunction in their day-to-day operations.

During the strategic planning meeting, the partners at one company wanted to clarify whether the real strategic objective was to maximize partners', clients', or associates' financial returns. Some advocated for the importance of one stakeholder over the others, while others proposed a balanced, multi-stakeholder objective.

In the end, this firm realized that while some prominent partners had been focusing on maximizing their personal wealth, the company's founding principles emphasized placing the customers' wealth first and foremost. Once they clarified their strategic intent, they were able to start realigning decisions, performance measures, and behaviors. The most significant change resulting from this greater strategic clarity was establishing a few measurable objectives aligned with the strategy.

Many leaders assume that setting financial goals is a sufficient strategy objective. A senior executive once told me: "After all, we are in the business of making money, that is the real strategic focus, all else is frosting on the cake." I was surprised to hear this as he was leading a company-wide performance improvement effort.

"Are you after any way possible of making money, or do you want to improve this organization's performance?" I asked him. "Both," he replied confidently. "Then, which one is most important to you right now?" I asked of him. "Money!" was his instinctive response. The performance improvement initiative at this company never took hold, and after 18 months, it was abandoned in favor of layoffs.

Pursuing shareholder value as the primary strategic focus has led leaders to make incorrect and often unethical decisions. This logic has encouraged unsustainable games to boost stock price, irresponsible accounting to show higher earnings, and mindless cost cutting to maintain profits.

Doing whatever it takes to make money is not a sound strategy. It is like the answer of the ambitious youth who, when asked what he wants to be when he grows up, says: "I want to make lots of money." While we can appreciate his drive, we are still not sure *how* he plans to achieve that goal. Defining the scope of *how* we serve customers is part of every clear strategy. A well-defined strategy describes *what* the objective is and *how* we will achieve that objective.

First say to yourself what you would be;
and then do what you have to do.

~Epictetus

Defining the Strategic Scope

The strategic scope defines whom we serve, where, and how. A company's scope identifies customers, offerings, and markets. The combination of these elements creates a unique value proposition to the customer.

Companies are best able to deliver value to customers and compete in the industry by defining a unique value proposition. Understanding who the customer is and is not helps companies avoid pursuing unprofitable or unsustainable markets. Providing product or service offerings that are precisely what the target customer wants drives the firm's market share.

Some strategy models encourage businesses to grow by expanding their market share. The logic is that the more customers they have, the better off they will be. The flaw with this line of reasoning is obvious: companies that simply pursue more customers often find themselves profiting the least.

Unless leaders focus on attracting the right customers, their businesses can become burdened with having to meet too many expectations they cannot effectively fulfill. Companies with a selective share of the market are often extremely profitable. A far better strategy is based on a clear sense of which customers we serve and the scope of our services.

WalMart and Costco illustrate two businesses that provide food, clothing, and a vast array of household items from furniture to electronics. Both are successfully competing by communicating clear and distinct value propositions.

Why would customers shop at WalMart *and* at Costco? You can find many of the same products at both stores. You may also think that you are getting a great value from each. So what is really different?

WalMart's value proposition can be stated as consistent low prices for a broad range of goods that are always in stock at convenient locations near the customer's home. WalMart concentrates on delivering value by providing a large selection of items; pursuing economies of scale; setting strict controls for suppliers on price, quantity, and on-time delivery; and building stores everywhere there is a large enough market. When WalMart identifies a product their customers want, it dominates the low-cost market with rigorous consistency.

On the other hand, Costco positions itself as providing a high quality selection of best-in-class products at a competitive price to members who enjoy the shopping experience. In order to deliver value, Costco sells larger amounts of key products only, changes their product mix and in-store product location to create a treasure-hunt feel in the store, and feeds their customers a wide variety of tasters. To reinforce the shopping experience, Costco pays higher wages to their employees and constantly trains them on customer service and product knowledge. The idea is that shopping at Costco will be a more pleasant experience and that as a valued member you will buy larger quantities and spend more per visit.

With clearly defined value propositions, each company is able to compete successfully in what can be broadly defined as the same industry. In fact, because of their clear differentiation, there is space for both stores in the same market. Even a small mom-and-pop convenience store can successfully compete with these two giants if it can define its unique value to the local community.

Such is the case of inner-city convenience stores that build close relationships with their customers and are conveniently located within walking distance. The employees recognize their customers by name. The stores offer special promotions on weekends and extend small credit amounts to regular customers between pay periods. Some of these stores further emphasize their unique value by offering a delivery service to nearby apartments at no additional charge.

The real threat of a WalMart or a Costco to the local convenience store owners may lie more in their ability to provide a unique value to their customers than on the size of the competitors. Businesses in all industries, regardless of size, fall prey to more assertive players if they operate without a clear value proposition. Being clear about what value you bring to customers is essential.

O would some power the gift to give us
to see ourselves as others see us.

~Robert Burns

Understanding Strategic Advantage

Strategic advantage means doing something that has distinctive value in the eyes of the customers. A firm that cannot explain why customers should buy its product or service is doomed to failure. Likewise, an organization that takes its customers for granted is an accident waiting to happen.

The reason some organizations find themselves in dire need of change in the first place is that they stopped listening to their customers. Most striking is how they justify their superior position. You can hear them talking about customers with contempt saying, "We need to educate the customer," "Often customers don't know what they want," "We will tell them what is best for them and they will have to buy it," or "Who do they think they are, anyway?"

The Change Masters set their course based on customer feedback. Before coming up with a new strategy, the 10 most successful changes sent out their executives to personally meet with employees and customers. Their fact-finding mission was to learn firsthand what was going on. They came back with plenty of ideas about areas needing to be fixed right away and over time. The essence of the strategy can be seen as a response to a current market need or latent opportunity.

In a legendary corporate turnaround, Lou Gerstner resurrected IBM from an all-but-certain death. In 1993, more than 90% of IBM's profits came from its mainframe sales, which were sinking fast. Conventional wisdom said that the mainframe was simply losing out to personal computers. Plans to break up IBM into smaller, supposedly more nimble businesses, were well underway when Gerstner arrived. "That made no sense to me," he said.

As a former customer of IBM and head of American Express's travel services division, Gerstner knew otherwise. It was true that customers no longer wanted to be locked into a single supplier like IBM for all their information technology needs. But neither did they relish the task of having to pick and choose from among thousands of suppliers to build a working system.

"Listen to customers—they know best what they need," Gerstner said to his IBM management team. You can't run a worldwide credit card business on a PC. You can't run an airline on a PC. Mainframes were still needed. IBM's problem, they learned from their customers, was not product but price.

As an IBMer myself, when I worked as an organizational researcher at the world corporate headquarters, one of my assignments was to analyze the results of IBM's market research survey. The feedback from customers essentially stated that IBM products were reliable and high quality, but they saw the IBM brand as expensive and inflexible. Customers complained most adamantly about IBM's high prices, which were inexplicably well above those of the competition.

Delivering that message to IBM executives was not fun. At meetings, feedback was not welcomed, because they had come to equate concern with distrust and dissent with dishonor. Critical customer feedback was intolerable, since IBM was used to telling customers what was best for them. "What do they expect?" one executive blasted during the feedback presentation. "We cannot possibly price ourselves with the clone makers." In those days, IBM, not Microsoft, was the biggest software company in the world, but none of the software IBM sold worked with anything other than IBM hardware. In fact, most IBMers disdainfully referred to all non-IBM computers simply as "clones."

Looking around at the observable symbols of power and prestige, no one doubted that responding to feedback was going to require a vastly different type of company than IBM was at that time. The company had become paralyzed by its own beliefs and assumptions. IBM was operating as if they still ruled the computer world. While at American Express, Gerstner recalled that he had heard of an IBM representative withdrawing all support for a massive credit card data center simply because the manager there had installed a single Amdahl computer in a facility that previously had been 100% IBM equipped.

After listening to the brutal facts, Gerstner then asked why the company hadn't lowered its prices to meet the competition. "Because we'll lose substantial revenues and profits when we need them badly," he was told. That was not exactly long-term thinking. "Get me a price-reduction plan in two weeks," Gerstner demanded. The idea that IBM, which used to control the computer market, had to actually compete for business was a rather shocking proposition.

The last thing IBM needs right now is a vision.
What it needs right now are tough-minded,
market-driven, highly effective strategies.

~Lou Gerstner, IBM, 1993

By this statement Lou Gerstner was not discarding the value of vision. IBM had a vibrant vision as a leader in its industry. That vision had inspired IBM over the decades to achieve a pre-eminent market position. What was desperately missing was a down-to-earth, reality-based plan to make good on that vision.

It took a disinterested outsider like Gerstner to break the back of the inbred culture. He knew he was there to do that job, so he decided to respond to the market needs quickly. He also sent out a steady stream of e-mails directly to IBM employees to keep them posted about what was going on. Most IBMers had little or no contact with the outside world of computer technology because they treated everything but IBM-made products with contempt.

By infusing a sense of urgency into the company, Gerstner led Big Blue from an $8 billion loss in 1993 to a $3 billion profit in 1994—an unprecedented $11 billion turnaround! IBM today is a vastly different company than it was only 15 years ago. It has transformed successfully, but it took drastic and painful measures. Becoming open to feedback helped IBM wake up to reality and change.

Feedback clarifies the value we bring to others. Feedback helps us become grounded in reality. We may not *want* to know how others see us, but we *need* to know the impact that our actions have on other people. Without feedback we are unable to improve our interactions with others. Proactively seeking feedback is the best way to stay in tune with reality.

> # Feedback clarifies the value we bring to others.

Feedback from relevant groups helps leaders see more clearly how others see their organization. It also shows the impact of their decisions on others. We can measure our views against those of others to visualize value gaps. Value gaps identify areas where a team is failing to deliver on an important attribute to another stakeholder group. Value gaps become opportunities to fulfill unmet expectations. They also point to vulnerable areas.

The most progressive organizations use stakeholder feedback as part of their strategic planning process. The feedback allows leaders to measure strategic alignment inside and outside the organization. Customers have a voice in the company's planning process as their feedback helps leaders understand what they value and to what extent the company is delivering that value.

In most industries, small gains in customer satisfaction lead to sizeable differences in the market. Take, for example, customer satisfaction in the automobile industry. Satisfaction surveys reveal that customers declare 82% satisfaction with their cars on average. The distance between the highest and lowest rated car companies in 2008 was only 11%, with the Lexus Division of Toyota Motor Corporation leading the industry with 87% satisfaction and Chrysler's Jeep at the other end of the spectrum with 76% satisfaction. A difference in customer satisfaction of only a few percentage points spell the difference between the best and those far behind.[21]

The customer defines the value we provide. Listening to the customer is the best way to clarify a business's strategic advantage in the market. Feedback holds a mirror in front of us that allows us to see what others are seeing. Feedback creates a felt need for change. To channel such a sense of urgency into action, we need a plan.

Nothing is particularly hard
if you can divide it into small jobs.

~Henry Ford

Planning the Implementation

A strategic plan defines how the organization is going to achieve its objectives. Translating the strategy into an action plan is the first step to putting the strategy to work.

The strategic planning process creates a hierarchy of objectives, going from general to specific. This approach lays out a logical sequence of events based on causes and effects. The strategic plan facilitates coordination of complex work, starting with the organization's strategic business objectives and then focusing on increasingly specific objectives.

This approach breaks down each objective into lower level goals. For any objective, the objective in a lower rank answers the question "How?" and the objective in a higher rank answers the question "Why?" Each objective has an owner who is the person ultimately responsible for the goal.

It is critical that even at the lowest levels of the organization, teams and individuals understand their business strategies. Moreover, they need to be able to articulate how their job contributes to the company's overall objectives. Supporting a strategy means little unless people commit to specific actions.

In a dynamic environment, planning and implementing becomes an interactive process. Leadership is distributed and decisions are made on the spot. Employees must make decisions based on experience, relying more on intuition than on exhaustive data analysis. Organizations depend on personal initiative and commitment more than on set roles and directions.

Without a strategic plan we cannot hope for people to commit to a change process. No matter how personally committed we are to the idea of change, managers and employees simply don't know what they are committing to do unless there is a specific plan. The plan carries us forward past good intentions and initial excitement, as long as we can develop commitment to the plan at all levels of the organization.

Everybody has a plan until they get hit in the face.

~Mike Tyson

The difficulty with implementing strategic change is not so much in the planning as it is in following through. Sooner or later we are all going to get hit in the face. What do we do then? Keep going! Don't let that distract you from pursuing your goals. There are countless reasons why people will question, delay, divert, or stall change. People commit to change when they voluntarily decide that is what they want to do.

Implementing a strategic plan requires building commitment, taking accountability, and following through. In order to foster commitment for change, leaders need to delegate responsibilities with the authority to carry them out. This requires a greater amount of autonomy, allowing individuals to decide how to achieve their goals and monitor their own progress. As initiative increases, resistance to change goes down.

I learned the value of delegating goal setting while working with an organization that was performing well below its strategic objectives. Several units were supposed to contribute to the overall goal for the organization and they all seemed fully committed to do so. However, no amount of training, coaching, or tracking measures seemed to close the gap between the goal and actual performance. At one point, we asked each unit to state their goal. To my surprise, their individual goals did not add up to the organization's total goal. It did add up, however, to their current level of performance. In their eyes, they were achieving *their* goals.

The following year, we reversed the process, encouraging a bottom-up goal-setting approach—challenging very low goals, if necessary, but letting each department and their leader set their own goals. We added up their individual goals to a grand total that was far higher than the organization's total the previous year. Where there was personal ownership and commitment, the goals were achieved.

No amount of tools and technology should reduce the human dimension of implementing a strategic plan. Tools and technology can enhance our ability to execute a plan, but they must not lessen the human element. Successful change maximizes the human characteristics to make the transition.

Facilitating the Transition

Our response to change depends on our role in it. Those who initiate change see it as an opportunity. Those who resist change tend to experience the situation as a threat. In order to be strategically agile, we have to become our own change champions.

In our lives we face changes that can produce threats or opportunities. The outcome depends on how we respond. The case of Ann and Mike illustrates a work situation many people today experience. Ann and Mike were working as internal auditors in their company's finance department. Their company had been around for many years and their jobs seemed secure. Lately, however, their department had been relying increasingly on external auditors for the more advanced technical work. Both Ann and Mike noticed their roles becoming less valuable relative to the roles of the external auditors.

Ann decided to bring more value to her job. She started by asking her manager how she could add more value and, with the help of a coach, created a development plan. She interviewed the external auditors to learn how to work more effectively with them. Ann discovered a need for playing an advisory role, translating business goals into specific projects for the external auditors. Ann talked to her manager to get additional education. She decided to attend conferences on the subject and took evening classes from the local university. In a matter of two years, Ann was certified as a financial advisor and began playing a more valuable role in the company.

Mike, on the other hand, focused on protecting his turf by performing his current job responsibilities to the best of his abilities. He often felt he was competing with external auditors for the more interesting work and tried hard to demonstrate that he could perform just as well—for a lot less than the expensive external consultants. At some point, he even cut off all communications with the external auditors because he saw them as the enemy. While Mike was still a competent worker, in many ways he had become a nay-sayer who often criticized and found errors with the work of the consultants. Senior managers avoided Mike because they considered him negative.

Within two years, the finance department completely outsourced all auditing work. Ann was promoted to director of strategic planning for one of the divisions. Mike lost his job.

Faced with the exact same situation, Ann created an opportunity, while Mike approached it as a threat. Over time, a gap formed between the former peers, leading to opposite outcomes. In the same ways, we create opportunities or threats by the way we approach the changes we face. Seizing the opportunity is essential to making the most from change.

He who cannot change the very fabric of
his thoughts will never be able to change reality,
and will never, therefore, make any progress.

~Anwar Sadat

Chapter Review

Summary

In a fast-changing world, plans quickly become obsolete, making strategic agility of greater value than relying on a set plan. Creating a strategic plan for change requires dynamic analysis and active planning for seizing the opportunities as they arise. People can be strategically agile when they clearly understand what the enterprise is trying to achieve. Understanding the objectives and the scope is essential to staying focused. Receiving regular feedback is crucial to understanding the value we bring. To be strategically agile, people need to understand who is responsible for doing what in the group.

Key Points

- In a changing world, strategic agility is required to seize opportunities for change.
- People can stay focused on the right priorities when they have concrete objectives.
- Regular feedback clarifies the team's unique value.
- Understanding who is responsible for doing what in the team allows people to make good choices.
- Implementing change requires that everyone understands the game plan.

Group Discussion

1. How do we describe our organization's strategy in simple terms?
2. What are our team's concrete strategic objectives?
3. What unique or distinctive value does our team provide?
4. Can we describe each team member's roles and responsibilities?

Access additional Ascent Tools at
www.ascent-advisor.com/tools.html

The Ascent Process
5Es for Mastering Change

Build Common Purpose	Clarify Direction	**Develop Capacity**	Inspire Commitment	Achieve Results
Envision	Evaluate	**Empower**	Engage	Evolve
What do we want to see happen?	How can we make it happen?	**How do we build on strengths?**	How do we inspire collaboration?	How do we track progress?

## CHAPTER SIX

Develop Capacity
Empower: How do we build on strengths?

*At the end of the day, you bet
on people, not on strategies.*

~Larry Bossidy

Making Wise People Choices

Vision provides the purpose and strategy the plan, but it is the people who make them happen. The first two steps in the Path of Ascent define "Why" and "What" we are to do. The next and third step identifies "Who" is going to do it.

There is an obvious interdependence between what we are to do and who is going to do it. Each decision influences the other. We need to know what we are doing before we can decide who is best qualified to do it. At the same time, who is involved determines what will actually get done.

When a vision and strategy are in place, assembling the right group of people becomes the most important step in determining the outcome. Get people driven for excellence on board, and they will achieve great results simply because that is their nature. On the other hand, surround yourself with mediocrity, and any plan, no matter how great, will fall to the level of the people involved.

Getting the right people in a team proves elusive for most leaders. The task is complicated because organizations have to juggle multiple positions, openings, transfers, promotions, and resignations simultaneously. What makes it most challenging is the complexity inherent in assessing people. The following are the five most common pitfalls leaders face in making good people choices:

1. Lacking the courage to address poor performance.
2. Difficulty making good assessments.
3. Feeling pressure to fill a position.
4. Difficulty attracting and retaining talent.
5. Avoiding the pain of ending an employment relationship.

Of the five, the most common problem is feeling uneasy about having an uncomfortable and potentially unpleasant conversation with an employee. Instead of addressing poor performance right away, many supervisors hold back. Most supervisors struggle for words to convey the resolve to get results while still caring for the person. If things turn out badly, they may fear losing the contributions the person is already making.

When supervisors find themselves going back and forth, trying to justify keeping a person, chances are good that they are avoiding a much needed conversation. A simple exercise can test whether you have the right people in your team. Draw a circle representing your ideal team. Outside the circle, list the names of each person currently working with you. Assume that they are not currently working with you. Draw an arrow for each person you want to bring back into circle. Those left out of the circle may not belong to the team.

Making poor hiring decisions, the second most common problem, reveals the difficulties of assessing a person objectively. The traditional interviewing process provides a protracted and inaccurate view of candidates. Both parties are trying to impress each other rather than trying to strike a fit. Interviews are filled with salesmanship, but very little critical assessment to get to the unvarnished truth. Unless organizations create a thorough hiring process that relies on objective selection criteria, costly hiring mistakes usually happen.

If the situation involves promoting employees within the organization, some supervisors prefer to pick those with whom they are comfortable, not necessarily the best qualified. The incumbent may not be the ideal candidate, but is usually a safer choice. In addition, most supervisors are uncomfortable hiring people who are better qualified than themselves; instead they tend to hire people they can more easily control.

Sometimes, leaders are under pressure to fill a position. They may rush through the interviews feeling too constrained by time to properly assess candidates. To compound the problem, the leaders may not have an adequate pool of qualified candidates. Leaders may feel additional strain if the position has been vacant due to hiring freezes or other delays. Under such pressure, leaders feel a real sense of urgency to get a person in the job as soon as possible. In the urge to get a body—anybody— leaders are more likely to see a fit for the position, even with little real evidence.

Another problem is that organizations struggle to attract or retain talent. Some companies place enormous demands on their employees to the point that the top talent leave. Under such circumstances, some supervisors assume that the organization is unable to attract the very best. If the recruiters and leaders are ready to settle for lesser talent, that's exactly what they are going to get.

Finally, the most heart-wrenching personnel decisions are often associated with firing employees. Firing an employee is inherently difficult, especially during a time of rising unemployment when the prospects of finding another job are dim. The terminated employee is likely to harbor ill feelings toward the manager and the company. After a termination, remaining employees often have a shaken confidence in their manager and the company.

To overcome these five common pitfalls, I recommend adopting the following five steps for making wise people choices.

Each step adds insights into the candidate's traits, clarifies relationship goals, and builds mutual respect.

1. Get Real

Get to know the real person with whom you will be working. Reveal appropriate information about yourself and learn as much as you can about the other person.

2. Probe Deeply

Be genuinely curious and appropriately inquisitive about the candidate. Rely on multiple assessments to better understand the candidate, such as personality tests, 360-degree feedback, behavioral interviewing, and a thorough work history profile.

3. Get a Second Take

Get an outside opinion from someone who is not affected by the decision. Some salient traits are easily seen from the distance, but too obvious to be noticed when up close with another person. Compare insider-outsider views.

4. Take Your Time

Why rush? Be thorough and systematic in the selection process. Have a rigorous process and follow it. Don't skip steps. The right candidate will appreciate it, and some of the poor choices will voluntarily drop out.

5. Keep it Open

Maintain a two-way open line of communication about performance. Don't let things fester. Strengthen the relationship by addressing performance regularly, describing how behaviors (good or bad) impact results.

Getting the right people in your team comes down to making good people choices. Experts estimate the cost of a bad hiring or promotion decision ranges from 20% to 200% of the position's annual salary, meaning an employee who stays less than a year can cost in excess of $500,000 after accounting for direct and indirect costs of employment.

Teams and organizations that systematically attract, develop, and promote great people rely on a rigorous selection process. The responsibility for assembling the right team rests squarely on the shoulders of the supervising leader. With so much at stake riding on people choices, it is best to rely on a talent review process.

There's something rare, something finer far, something much more scarce than ability. It's the ability to recognize ability.

~Elbert Hubbard

Assembling the Right Team

On a flight from Los Angeles to New York City, I sat next to UCLA Basketball Coach Ben Howland. He was on his way to that year's draft at the Madison Square Garden. On his way, while sitting in the plane, he was incessantly exchanging phone calls with prospective players, rival coaches, and a slew of advisors. It was very interesting to experience the intensity of the process.

"This kid is really fast and can play the entire game without getting tired," Coach Howland would say over his phone while holding the sports page of the newspaper right in front of him. "We want him in at all costs, because we need speed in the team." Then, switching to another phone call, he would engage with the player, "You say you've got good offers, I'm sure we can match your best offer. But the real question you should be asking yourself is, which is the right team for you?"

After a brief exchange with the player, he would switch again, to a third call. "That kid has leadership skills. He can talk with the other players. He is positive and uplifting. I know there are better players, but I want him in. We need a leader."

Once Coach Howland could no longer talk on the phone because the plane was ready to take off, he turned to me and said: "This is pretty crazy, isn't it?" I nodded in acknowledgment. "The key to getting the right team," he said, "is not just getting all the best players, but getting the right players for the team."

In sports as in other arenas, assembling the right team of people is a dynamic challenge. It requires understanding the interaction between members. It is about forming the group's

> **Building the right team
> is not about getting all
> the best players, but
> getting the right
> players for the team.**

character by blending a complementary set of individual traits. Whether you are assembling a sports team, organizing a community service task force, or building a functional department at work, the talent review is a proven process for assembling the right team.

The talent review is the strategic people inventory that aligns people with strategy. It requires assessment, discussion, and decisions on people's roles, development needs, and future opportunities. All key players participate in the process, including additional high-potential candidates from inside or outside the organization who are nominated by the supervisor. For a small team, the review is conducted with all team members present. For larger organizations, the leadership group initially reviews the assessment results and then shares the information with each participant.

The talent review starts with defining what core competencies the organization needs to deliver its objectives. Defining a team's core competencies requires a strategic view of the role of the team now and in the future. Core competencies represent the essential set of knowledge, talent, skills, and experiences required to succeed. The core competencies cannot be compromised without compromising the team's objectives.

Once the team has defined what competencies they absolutely need, they assess what talent they currently have. Collecting information from multiple sources, the talent assessment includes the candidate's track record, leadership qualities, and growth potential. A combination of psychometric tests, survey

Assembling the Right Team

COMPETENCIES
Define the team's
core competencies

TEAM PROFILE
Assess the team's
current talent profile

GAPS
Identify competency gaps
Decide how to close the gaps

ALIGNMENT
Align people's strengths
to the team's core competencies

feedback, and behavioral interviews is required to obtain this information.

The results of the individual talent assessments are consolidated into a team talent profile. This report provides a view of the group's overall talent, bench strength, and development needs. The team talent profile displays an aggregate of individual results across core dimensions. It also shows individual scores, highlighting specific strengths and areas that need improvement.

A review of each person's talent assessment provides the critical input necessary for making strategic people decisions. During the talent review meeting, the team paces through each person's profile, one at a time. This review facilitates a meaningful and informed discussion about each player relative to the team needs.

The outcome of talent review is to align people's strengths with the team's competencies. Identifying each person's achievements, relationships, and growth potential provides a good inventory of what talent the team has. Aligning that talent pool with the team's core competencies may reveal gaps—areas where the team is currently underperforming simply because of lack of talent.

It is the team leader who ultimately decides how members contribute to the team. The role of the leader is to allocate resources and development opportunities and take personnel actions. The decisions to retain, grow, engage, and resolve specific individuals have a direct and immediate impact on the team performance. The process accelerates change as the right people are placed where they are needed.

The persons being assessed receive their talent profiles: positive reinforcement, development opportunities, or performance improvement plans. In every case, individuals complete their development plan as a result of the talent review. If a plan already exists, the talent review provides an update of their plan in advance of the performance appraisal.

Not every person will fit perfectly into the defined team's competencies. Individuals who cannot be easily aligned with core competencies may deserve additional attention. There may be different perceptions of the person's contributions. The person may act differently in different settings or contribute in ways that are not well aligned with the team. The talent review helps clarify the person's contribution as well as the organization's needs.

There are cases when a person does extremely well in some areas and very poorly in others. For example, a person who is highly competent at getting results but is difficult to work with presents one of the greatest challenges. This person can be highly valued for getting things done and achieving goals. At the same time, his actions may frustrate others to the point that long-term effectiveness is seriously compromised.

Looking solely at this person's results, he can be labeled as a top performer. Yet, considering his strained relationships and communication style, he can be deemed a low performer. If results come at too high a cost, many will question the real value of those results.

How an organization deals with such a person defines what the leader ultimately wants. This single decision sets the precedent for what others in the team can and cannot do without consequences. If leaders keep and even protect this person, they are proving by their actions that they want results at any cost. On the other hand, if leaders put up with the bad behavior, they indicate that they are willing to settle for mediocre performance. Ideally, the leader would require the person to change the poor conduct while recognizing the achievements.

To illustrate how the process works, we can review the case of Brian, the director of operations at a fast growing firm. Brian exuded confidence about his prominent position and solid track record with the firm. Only a few years before he had been brought into the company by a former supervisor who was now the company's vice president. Brian quickly gained a reputation as a manager able to able to get things done, leading the largest department in the company. He approached his talent review with visible confidence, knowing that the company relied heavily on him.

At one point during the talent interview Brian confessed, "If others don't perform for me, we get into a screaming match, and then they know they have to do it." "Do you think that is an effective way of getting people to do their best?" the interviewer asked. "It works for me," Brian replied, self assured. "Does it work for them over time?" the interviewer asked back. "As long as they get the job done, it doesn't matter to me," he replied abruptly. Brian's talent review revealed that he often acted as a bully, creating divisions and distrust among peers and direct reports.

At the talent review meeting, each executive presented their leaders in light of their recent working experiences and the results of the talent assessments. The group efficiently worked through the list of key players and usually agreed readily on most assessments. Most individual contributions aligned well with the organization's core competencies. Some individuals' talent profiles, however, required additional discussion, and the individuals were recommended for other roles.

Brian's vice president recommended him as a top performer. "He's great. He is fantastic," said Brian's supervisor as he placed Brian's profile in the Top Performer pile. "In what ways?" asked the company's president. Taken by surprise, the supervisor went on defending Brian with glowing generalities. Other senior managers pressed for details. "What leadership qualities do you see in him?" He couldn't be specific. His peers reported incidents that brought Brian's effectiveness into question and the vice president's face turned crimson.

After discussing Brian's leadership style, the group determined that while he had potential, he was not yet the type of leader the organization wanted as an example. His profile was placed on the side without a specific resolution. With some coaching and preparation, the vice president explained to Brian that he needed to face some feedback.

Brian's performance was great and the company greatly valued his contributions, but his style needed improvement. As Brian received the news, he went through several emotions. Finally, he accepted the challenge to work with a coach to develop his leadership style. Brian's vice president learned a valuable lesson about what was expected of leaders at this company. He became more aware of the value his peers placed on how tasks were accomplished.

The talent review helped this leadership team define specific qualities of the people they want to hire, fire, promote, and develop. The talent review process conducted by functional departments and work groups helped them account for the strengths and deficiencies of current players, uncover competency gaps, and mitigate risks in key positions. The process highlighted individuals who demonstrated potential for higher responsibilities and helped leaders make informed decisions about key resources.

Back to Coach Howland's comment that getting the best possible team is far more important than getting the best players. An impressive array of "A-Players" does not necessarily make for an "A-Team." A-Players may win games, but A-Teams win championships. In reviewing the team's talent profile, one needs to keep in mind how the players complement each other. The most important consideration is selecting the right team leader.

I look for three things in hiring people. The first is integrity, the second is intelligence, and the third is a high energy level. But, if you don't have the first, the other two will kill you.

~Warren Buffett

Empowering the Leader

The fastest way to set things going in a new direction is to empower a new leader. The rise of a newly appointed senior executive marks the start of the change period at each of the 50 transforming organizations studied. For better or for worse, the choice of a leader is the single most influential decision affecting the future and fortune of an entire organization. Change the leader and the entire organization shifts direction.

Take, for example, the role of Carlos Ghosn in transforming Nissan. Decades of rigid management and failure to respond to customer needs resulted in a $22 billion debt, declining market share, escalating dealer costs, and failing new car models. Nissan was on the brink of bankruptcy. Ghosn, a former Renault executive, was brought in to lead the battered company. He stated bluntly that Nissan was in "bad shape" and if he was to turn the company around, he needed to be in the driver's seat. There must be "no sacred cows, no taboos, and no constraints," Ghosn warned as he unveiled his plan for change at a Nissan management conference.[22]

Ghosn's direct and decisive management style stunned Nissan executives and quickly infused the company with a heavy dose of reality. Ghosn led an aggressive transformation by cutting costs, streamlining operations, and revitalizing the product lines. In the process, Ghosn reworked Nissan's rigid and hierarchical Japanese management style by bringing in a more direct and expeditious French-style culture that brought much needed transparency and action.

Under Ghosn's leadership, a more diverse management team struck at the heart of many of Japan's cherished corporate practices. One change, for example, was to require that both Japanese and non-Japanese managers be measured equally for performance, something that Nissan had not been doing. Successful managers received bonuses and stock options based strictly on results, and those who were unable to perform were let go.

Effective transformation leaders change themselves in the process of bringing about change in others. As leaders adopt the positive traits of the host culture, others more willingly embrace their ideas. Ghosn, who speaks fluent French, English, and Portuguese—but until his assignment to head Nissan spoke hardly a word of Japanese—surprised Nissan employees by delivering, in Japanese and without notes, an impassioned appeal asking them to join the effort to save their company. While his decisions shook many tenets of Japanese corporate culture, Ghosn's respect for the company's strengths made him a widely accepted leader at Nissan and by the Japanese people.

In a similar vein, James McNerney's involvement in 3M's turnaround demonstrates the impact of the leader. One of the United States' longest standing and strongest corporations, 3M is known for innovative products ranging from Post-it Notes® to fiber optics. Decades of sustained success resulted in corporate complacency, so that by 2000, 3M was stuck in an unbreakable pattern of stagnating market share and declining profits. McNerney, a former General Electric executive, was the first person in the company's 98-year history brought from the outside to lead 3M.

Within weeks of his appointment, McNerney announced plans to eliminate slower growing businesses, like low cost sandpaper products, in favor of faster growing ones, like health care devices. In the process, over 5,000 Minnesota employees lost their jobs. Long-time 3M employees had become accustomed to assuming that everybody would be taken care of as long as they did their jobs, even referring to the company as a maternal corporation that took care of its flock. That attitude disappeared soon after McNerney came in.[23]

Analysts pointed out that for 3M to grow, it had to change the way it did business. McNerney agreed, but he made sure to build on what was good about 3M's culture, and change only what was no longer sustainable. As a result, much of 3M's dedicated and hard-working culture became even stronger.

"My objective is to participate with growing this company," he said. "The onus is on me to become part of this rather than to come here with some big-fix plan, nothing could be farther from the truth. It's not about what needs fixing. It's a matter of building on this [company's] huge potential," McNerney told a news conference.[24]

The stories of Carlos Ghosn at Nissan and James McNerney at 3M illustrate the instrumental role of leaders in bringing about change. They set new standards and practices that effectively transformed their organizations. People used to a way of doing things had to reach beyond their comfort zones to meet the leader's goals. In turn, these leaders changed themselves, embracing what was good and valuable about the organization's culture.

Just like large international corporations, any group of people—teams, departments, and functions—respond to the influence of the group leader. The leader's standards are easily adopted by the rest of the group. Even societies rise or fall to the standards of their leaders. The values the leader promotes are as influential as the weaknesses they condone. In that sense, team performance rises no higher than that of their leaders.

**Team performance
rises no higher than
the leader's.**

In each of the 50 organizations studied, the unique traits and abilities of their leaders determined the direction, decisions, and actions taken. The best way to understand what took place at these 50 organizations is not to look at their business strategies,

Leaders of the Change Masters

#	Company	Transformation Leader	Key Contribution	Origin
1	Intel	Andrew Grove	Disciplined execution	Insider
2	Apple	Steve Jobs	Product innovation	Insider
3	General Electric	Jack Welch	Results driven growth	Insider
4	IBM	Lou Gerstner	Customer focused change	Outsider
5	Caterpillar	James W. Owens	Global expansion	Insider
6	McDonald's	James A. Skinner	Improved image	Insider
7	VeriSign	Vernon Irvin	Distinctive features	Insider
8	Nissan	Carlos Ghosn	Operational efficiency	Outsider
9	3M	James McNerney	Improved performance	Outsider
10	Xerox	Anne M. Mulcahy	Renewed credibility	Insider

organization structures, work processes, or human resource policies. It is the people that made all the difference! In a surprising way, this broad study of organizational change quickly became a study of leadership traits.

The Leaders of the Change Masters chart describes the key contributions each leader made during the change period. One can predict the direction of change simply by knowing the traits and style of the leader. In a remarkable way, their leadership strengths became the organization's focus for change.

An interesting insight from the Leaders of the Change Masters chart is that transforming an organization did not require bringing someone from the outside. Insiders are more often the successful change leaders, mainly because they are already well acquainted with the organization's culture, industry, and operations. As the chart shows, 7 out of 10 transformation leaders were insiders, often groomed and prepared for decades to succeed in their leadership roles. Conversely, the organizations that failed to change relied more often on outsiders.

Each Leader of the Change Masters played a distinctive role in defining the *need* for change. Seven of the 10 Change

Masters were in dire need for a turnaround to avoid an imminent bankruptcy. Their newly appointed leaders quickly redirected people's attention to a new set of priorities. However, not all successful changes were the result of a crisis. General Electric, McDonald's, and Caterpillar, for example, were experiencing substantial success. They had no issues pressing them to change. Yet their leaders were able to frame the need for improvement as a competitive challenge. While each company's need for and approach to change is unique, all companies that successfully navigate change have one thing in common: They effectively rallied people in support of change.

The pattern of failed change at the Change Failures is linked to leaders whose strengths were not in leading change. They may have been great managers and may have even led successful operations under different conditions. But when it came to change, they resisted it themselves.

Unsuccessful change leaders expected others to change without committing themselves to the course they prescribed. Rather than leading, they managed the change process. Rather than acting decisively, they endlessly talked about it. Over time, resistance to change grew stronger, resulting in turf battles, finger-pointing, and lack of any substantial improvement.

In the case of Nortel Networks (described at the beginning of this book), Dave House was purposely brought in to lead change, but he was not empowered. He was never given the authority necessary to make the change happen. Without the authority, he could not make the changes he had been hired to make.

Changing an organization is not the act of a single person. Effective leaders empower everyone across the organization to carry out their decisions. They start by earning the commitment of those who have influence, particularly formal and informal leaders involved in a change process. The combined effect of these key players is what ultimately transforms the character of an entire organization.

Understanding the types of resistance to change facing the initiative helps leaders gain support. The sponsor profile model identifies the levels of influence and commitment for change

Sponsor Profile

Roles of Key Players based on their Level of
Influence and Commitment for Change

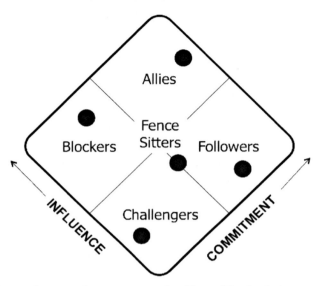

among key players in an organization. Each dot represents a person. Understanding their position, leaders can decide how to best approach each situation.

The four sponsor profiles describe roles individuals play in the change process. A sufficient proportion of Allies greatly increases the likelihood of success. At least one strong Ally is required to sponsor a successful change. Building a network of Allies is one of the key roles of an effective change leader. But a truly effective leader does not stop with enlisting the help of Allies. They work toward bringing everyone along!

Followers are friendly supporters willing to lend their votes. As a group, they can be helpful in swaying the public opinion. Broadening the scope of Followers helps persuade Fence Sitters, which are the more likely converts. Some Fence Sitters, however, will choose to remain neutral.

Challengers, by themselves, account for a passive opposition, but if organized as a group, they can voice significant resistance for change. The best approach for gaining support from

Challengers is by inviting them to participate, listening to their concerns, and clarifying their misconceptions.

Blockers are decidedly opposed to the change and will likely use their influence to prevent its progress. If identified, their impact can be anticipated and managed. Otherwise, the impact of invisible Blockers can prove fatal. The best strategy for dealing with a strong presence of Blockers is to actively include them as part of a coalition, giving them a stake in the outcomes, building on areas of agreement, and negotiating for degrees of support. Having a common purpose and a shared story of success will more readily persuade Blockers to become Allies.

On the Path of Ascent, resistance to change is seen as natural, necessary, and desirable. Differences of opinion are welcomed. Such differences do not represent an impediment to change, but rather a creative tension. The role of opposition helps refine the original means and ends. In this sense, the Path of Ascent takes a very different view than the traditional approach, which attempts to squelch the opposition.

An up-close look into the 10 most successful transformations reveals that, far from imposing change from an authoritarian standpoint, these companies involved an increasing number of people in the process. Rather than leveraging the leader's authority, these organizations empowered groups of influential people across the board. In fact, the Change Masters became talent factories by attracting, promoting, and developing an impressive workforce. Their approach was truly empowering.

Never believe that a few caring people can't change the world.
For, indeed, that's all who ever have.

~Margaret Mead

Empowering Change Champions

How does an organization, made up of multiple departments and functions, go about adopting new skills and practices? The fastest and most effective way to build widespread capacity is to empower change champions. It takes only a small amount of yeast to cause a whole loaf of bread to rise. Likewise, a relatively small group of people can provide the ferment to change an entire organization. Their unusual amount of influence comes from being insiders empowered with advanced knowledge and skills. The contagious transfer happens by example as these individuals work alongside with others. Acting as change champions, these specialists spread their know-how and disseminate innovative practices through the organization.

That is how Rick Van Poole became one of the unsuspected change champions at Crown Packaging. Rick was an up-and-coming star at Crown, rising quickly through the ranks to become a promising general manager. Rick's practical experience and natural intelligence had served him well, but his limitations held him and his organization back. When a market downturn left the company facing unprecedented challenges, Tom James, the company's COO, asked Rick to join a newly formed strategic implementation (SI) team. Joining the SI team was not precisely a welcomed move for Rick at first, since this team was one of the most vulnerable positions at the time.

Still, the SI team provided Rick a unique opportunity to expand his management expertise as he and the rest of the SI team members immersed themselves in an intensive training and certification process, where they were exposed to a variety of leadership training, survey feedback, 360-degree coaching, strategic planning methods, and quality controls. Team members also studied and then taught others concepts from the best management books. In a matter of months, the SI team members had acquired an impressive set of new skills, practices, and behaviors.

After completing their training, the SI team's task was to help various operations within the company improve quality, increase productivity, and reduce costs. They started with one of the operations that needed the most improvement. Working alongside workers at the target operation, Rick put his newly acquired skills to use with vigor. The entire SI team focused on achieving success at this one operation. The plant management and the employees gave them full support, and in a matter of months, productivity not only improved, it shot to record levels. Soon the plant was operating at break even and projecting profits in the near future.

The first big success for the SI team gave them credibility to move into other areas of the organization. Other divisions started requesting their help, and within months, several operations were seeing positive results.

As demand for their services grew, the size of the SI team expanded. Progressive employees volunteered to join the SI team and receive the training. The original members became master trainers. Overtime, as the expertise of SI team members became widely adopted across the organization, their tools and methods became the way of doing things and not just a program. The roles of the SI team members evolved from being seen as experts to becoming on-the-floor agents for change. After his eye-opening experience changing Crown's culture, Rick went on to buy a struggling company and turn it into a successful enterprise using the same approach.

This story illustrates how a relatively small group of people empowered with advanced knowledge and skills can influence an entire organization to change. The pattern of change champions became plainly evident as I compared the successful transformation of the Change Masters with their counterparts.

The Change Masters effectively deployed change champions. They relied on groups of highly skilled people to introduce sustainable improvements. This skilled force represented a mix of internal managers and external experts who were given specialized training and visible roles. As their expertise became widely adopted, their roles eventually integrated back into the formal structure of the organization.

The Change Failures made attempts at deploying change champions. However, their influence was limited. The level of specialization or the visibility of their roles was insufficient. More often, however, the change agent model was not properly implemented. In the failed changes, the agents for change remained experts (outsiders or members of a specialized department) that never fully integrated into the mainstream organization.

To illustrate the vital importance of having the change champions work along side the common worker, let's review China's use of "barefoot doctors." During Mao Zedong's rule, the Chinese health ministry had repeatedly failed to provide even the basic health care to the country's massive population. Disease in the rural regions was widespread and uncontrollable. The answer to this problem came in the form of empowered villagers.

Thousands of peasants, both men and women, were selected for a six months of intensive medical training to become primary healthcare providers in their villages. After being taught basic health principles, they were sent back to promote basic hygiene, preventive health care, and treat common illnesses. Barefoot doctors continued their farming work in the rice paddies, while being readily available to help those in need. In short time these change champions effectively stopped the spread of infectious diseases throughout rural China.[25]

> # A group of respected insiders empowered with new knowledge and skills influences the entire organization.

Change happens when an organization empowers a group of respected members with expertise to act as agents for change. The influence of this relatively small group of individuals transfers new knowledge, skills, and behaviors to the rest of the organization. As they work alongside others, they impart their expertise, which others adopt from observing their example. As they integrate into the fabric of the organization, people embrace a new way of doing things.

Go to the people.
Learn from them.
Love them.
Start with what they know.
Build on what they have.

> *But of the best leaders,*
> *when their task is accomplished*
> *and their work is done,*
> *the people will remark:*
> *"We have done it ourselves."*
>
> ~ 2,000-Year-Old Chinese Poem

Empowering One's Self

Empowerment, ultimately, is a personal choice. We can empower others with authority, knowledge, and skills, but it is up to each person to receive the opportunity to empower one's self. The choice to be empowered is life-changing.

Irma Ramos made her life-changing decision when she decided to step up to lead her team. At the age of 18, Irma started working as an administrative assistant to the founding partners of a fast-paced financial services firm in New York City. As the company grew, Irma was happy to learn new responsibilities.

I met Irma while facilitating a leadership development process with her company. During the course of the workshop, it became apparent that Irma was qualified and had the opportunity to move up to a manager role. Much was expected of whoever took that position, but Irma was unsure she really wanted the additional responsibilities of management. Besides, she felt inadequate and ill-prepared for the position, having no formal education in business. I frankly told Irma that there was about a 50% chance she would succeed as a manager. Taking a risk was part of the opportunity.

After some deliberation, Irma decided to take on the challenge of the manager role. This required her to redefine her relationships with her peers and gain the confidence of others at the company as a credible leader. She set out to learn as much as she could about leadership while being coached by her supervisor.

Progress was slow initially, but within six months, Irma did what no one at the company had done: she went from entry-level administrative support to a management role. She earned the respect and support of other managers, including the partners at the firm. Irma encouraged her staff to advance their skills and obtain certifications. She also facilitated leadership group discussions with the managers at the company.

With a renewed sense of confidence, Irma then made other important decisions that broadened her horizons. One of them is that she arranged for the care of a homeless woman. Irma had passed Natalie on the streets of Manhattan every day on her way to work. She had chatted with her and given her occasional handouts and homemade meals. But now Irma took the next step: she called social services and arranged for Natalie to be at a psychiatric hospital, where she received a haircut, clean clothes, and eventually moved to a permanent and safe place to live. Irma continues to visit with Natalie about every month and cheerfully admits that "Natalie has made me a better person."

We empower ourselves by putting our strengths to work. As we do that, we become the source of positive changes in our lives and in the lives of others. Empowering ourselves and others in the organization bring out the best in everyone.

As is our confidence, so is our capacity.

~ William Hazlitt

Chapter Review

Summary

Change happens when the right group of people is empowered to lead. This starts by assembling the right team. Aligning the team's core competencies with the talents of individual members identifies the resources a team has and needs. Empowering the change leader is the single most important decision affecting the direction of change. Leaders empower change champions to build the organization's capacity through advanced knowledge and skills. Ultimately, empowerment is a personal choice to step up and make a greater contribution.

Key Points

- Successful change hinges on making good people choices, requiring that we really get to know the other person well.
- To assemble the right team, compare the team's core competencies with the strengths of each member.
- The influence and commitment of the leader is key to a successful change.
- Change champions facilitate the widespread adoption of new practices.
- While we can empower others, it is ultimately up to each person to empower himself or herself.

Group Discussion

1. Do we have the right individuals to achieve the team's objectives?
2. How can we be more effective at selecting the right person for the job?
3. How can we increase our team's influence and commitment for change?
4. How can we best influence the organization's capacity?

Access additional Ascent Tools at
www.ascent-advisor.com/tools.ht ml

The Ascent Process
5Es for Mastering Change

Build Common Purpose	Clarify Direction	Develop Capacity	Inspire Commitment	Achieve Results
Envision	Evaluate	Empower	**Engage**	Evolve
What do we want to see happen?	How can we make it happen?	How do we build on strengths?	**How do we inspire collaboration?**	How do we track progress?

## CHAPTER SEVEN

Inspire Commitment
Engage: How do we inspire collaboration?

Individual commitment to a group effort—
that is what makes a team work,
a company work, a society work.

~Vince Lombardi

Engaging in a Common Cause

Today's work force faces daunting challenges to cut costs, improve quality, and develop new products and services in an increasingly competitive world. One key element common to the companies that succeed is commitment and teamwork. Achieving high levels of teamwork and commitment was key to the turnaround at Xerox.

Anne Mulcahy became the accidental CEO of the company she had worked for all of her career. Taking her first job after college as a Xerox sales representative, she worked her way up the management ranks over 35 years, marrying and having a family along the way with Joe Mulcahy, a Xerox sales executive. One day, as she was preparing for a business trip to Japan, she was asked instead to consider taking the company's top position.

"I never expected to be CEO, nor was I groomed to be CEO. It was a total surprise to everyone, including me," said Mulcahy. At that time she just wanted to go home to discuss the decision with her family. Her husband and children gave her their full support.[26] She accepted the job and was handed the reins of a company heading for bankruptcy.

"Nothing spooked me so much as waking up in the middle of the night and thinking about 96,000 employees and retirees and what would happen if this thing went south. Entire families worked for Xerox."[27] Her advisers urged Mulcahy to declare bankruptcy in order to clear Xerox of its $18 billion debt, but she resisted. "Bankruptcy is never a win," she told them. In fact, she concluded that resorting to bankruptcy to escape debt could make matters worse for Xerox in the long run. Instead, she chose a much more difficult and risky goal—restoring to greatness the company she loved so much.

Mulcahy's early sales experiences helped her develop skills in building teams, setting goals, and keeping employees and customers feeling good about the company. Her first goal as CEO was to build a strong leadership team. Obviously, not everyone was supportive of her appointment at first. She didn't have time for playing politics. Without delay, she met personally with the top 100 executives to gain their support. She let them know how dire the situation was and asked them if they were prepared to commit. "This has got to be about the company," she explained to them. "So we're totally in sync, or you need to go." Ninety-eight of the 100 executives decided to stay and give their support to pull the company out of the crisis.

Mulcahy then sent her team off to gather feedback by meeting in person with groups of employees and major customers. She wanted everyone to fully understand what was going on and get a grasp of the situation. They heard plenty of complaints from both groups and did their best to build their confidence. Customer trust was harder to win because many feared Xerox might not be around to fulfill their orders. Mulcahy galvanized the sales force and built customer confidence by making good on the promise that she would fly anywhere to save any customer.

Despite the tremendous pressures the company was under, Mulcahy made people publicly accountable for setting realistic expectations and delivering on promises. She talked openly about the company's situation and engaged others in dialogue. She wanted people to discuss problems and come to resolutions. In meetings, she often acted as a facilitator, allowing for different views to be aired and pulling things together at the end. She kept stressing the importance of everyone working together.

"Month after month there was not a single piece of good news. We asked ourselves, could it get any worse? Yes. And it did." Through the bad days, Mulcahy drew inspiration by interacting with fellow employees. She was at her best milling around, visiting with employees, listening to their stories, and sharing their passion for making a contribution. She was energized by the employees' enthusiasm and, in turn, her visits gave the employees a much needed dose of confidence in the company's future.

The leadership team banded together and became extremely supportive of each other; often exchanging encouraging comments. One such message came at a point when Mulcahy had flown back from Japan only to find it had been a dismal day at the office. Late in the evening, she came to the point that she did not know where to turn. For some reason, she decided to check her voicemail. The chief strategist, Jim Firestone, had left her a message: "This may seem like it's the worst day, hopefully it is, but we believe in you. This company will have a great future. Let tomorrow be a good day." That's just what she needed to hear to go on.

What Mulcahy cared most about was building a good team to lead the company. Despite tight budgets, she rewarded those who stuck it out, continued giving out raises, encouraged celebrating personal events with perks, and gave frequent recognition. Employees responded to Mulcahy's engaging leadership style. The company began feeling more like a team. People fought and debated, but at the end of the day, they pulled together for a common cause.

Meanwhile, the bankruptcy drumbeats continued as the company reported significant losses, used up its entire $7 billion line of credit, and watched its credit ratings drop sharply.

Making matters worse, the company was facing a massive investigation by the Securities and Exchange Commission for past billing and accounting practices.

Mulcahy didn't blink. She refused to cut back on research and development or field sales. Instead, she went after Xerox's bloated infrastructure, reached a painful settlement with the SEC for practices for which she was not responsible, and sold off pieces of the business. Along the way, she had to eliminate 28,000 jobs and billions in expenses. She implored employees to save every dollar as if it were their own. In the end, Mulcahy did a lot more than saving Xerox. She led a team to reinvent themselves and the company where they worked.[28]

Not every Transformation Leader has the personal touch of Anne Mulcahy. However, all successful transformations have engaged employees in the cause of change. The driver of engagement was meeting the challenge at hand. In order to pull it off, every leader and employee had to commit, heart and soul, to something greater than themselves. As a result, people in these organizations became more united, pulled together, and achieved extraordinary results.

Ultimately, these changes were successful because the organizations changed their culture. The chart below describes the culture change at each of the Change Masters. Despite all the financial pressures and emotional distress, the people working

Culture Change
of the Change Masters

#	Company	Period	Driver of Cultural Change
1	Intel	1994-1999	Leader of computer microprocessors
2	Apple	2001-2005	Innovative i-products for the mobile Internet age
3	General Electric	1995-1999	Undisputed market leader in chosen industries
4	IBM	1995-1999	Leader of high-end systems and services
5	Caterpillar	2003-2007	Resilient and entrepreneurial global expansion
6	McDonald's	2003-2006	Reinvent as a health conscious and socially responsible brand
7	VeriSign	2003-2006	Distinctive electronic commerce technology
8	Nissan	2000-2004	Shift into innovative and quality cars
9	3M	2000-2004	Improved quality and productivity
10	Xerox	2001-2005	Innovator in smart document technology

for these companies had a cause. Employees were able to rally around a common cause that made the pain of changing worth every sacrifice.

A common driver for cultural change never quite took root at the Change Failures. Leaders at the Change Failures gave speeches, created catchy slogans, launched motivational campaigns, and sponsored incentive programs, but failed to connect with the average worker. The prevailing sentiment was that they were not in it together. The essential relationship between management and employees remained transactional and accusatory. As things got tougher, the gap between these groups widened. The companies that failed to change did not engage people in transforming themselves or the company.

> ## We become fully engaged when we commit to a cause greater than ourselves.

Culture isn't just one aspect of the game. It is the game.

~Lou Gerstner

Tapping Into Hearts and Minds

Leaders have always known that it is through people—their employees mainly—that they achieve the desired business results. After all, it is people who design the products, drive the equipment, and sell the services. When all other factors level the playing field, the most engaged teams outperform the competition.

Engagement is the cause that energizes people to work together as a team. Engagement is the voluntary dedication to doing one's very best work. When people apply their hearts and minds to what they do, they become engaged. They take pride in their organization, feel committed to serving others, and make good on their promises.

Intuitively, we all know engagement when we see it. When people are motivated and effective at work, the team climate is different. Customers sense it immediately as they talk on the telephone with a customer representative, or as they try to return an item or ask a question of a store clerk. Consider what ordinary people who are engaged willingly do when no one is watching:

- A sales person works late into the evening after reaching his personal quota to help a colleague secure a deal that helps achieve the team's revenue goal.
- A machine operator stays a few additional hours after checking out from his shift to coach his counterpart in a new production system.
- A retail employee goes to a customer's residence to personally deliver an exchanged item and make sure a complaint gets resolved to the customer's satisfaction.
- A manager takes time to personally congratulate a new hire for completing an important project on time and gives that person a coupon for her favorite drink.
- An emergency room nurse comes up with a more efficient process that re-routes incoming patients so they receive service faster, and the ER can take care of more patients.

What is common to all these situations is *engagement!*

Just how engaged are you at work? Your level of engagement determines your performance. If you are anywhere below fully engaged, chances are that you are not giving your best at work. You are depriving yourself, your team, and your customers of the best you can offer.

If we are anything less than fully engaged, we are depriving ourselves and others from the value work is meant to create. The value of being fully engaged at work is a mutual benefit to the employee, the employer, and the customer. To the employee, engagement means a more fulfilling job. To the employer, engagement translates into retention and productivity. To the customer, engagement means better quality and service.

A crucial aspect of engagement is that it simultaneously meets the needs of the business and the people. Meeting the enterprise performance objectives while creating a more fulfilling working environment is what makes engagement so valuable. A growing body of research links employee engagement to business performance metrics.

Towers Perrin (ISR) found that high engagement firms experienced a growth rate of 28% earnings per share, compared with a decline of 11.2% for low engagement firms.[29] Gallup's research indicates that public organizations ranking in the top quartile of employee engagement had earnings per share growth of 2.6 times the rate of companies whose engagement is below average.[30] Studies of call centers show a clear link between employee and customer satisfaction.[31] Apparel and home furnishings retailer JCPenney found that "stores with top quartile engagement scores generate about 10% more in sales per square foot than average and 36% more operating income than similar-sized stores in the lowest quartile."[32]

The Society for Human Resources Management (SHRM) reports the impact of employee engagement at the brewing company MolsonCoors, estimating that by strengthening employee engagement, the company saved $1,721,760 in one year alone. As part of this estimate, they found that the average cost of a safety incident for engaged employees was $64 compared with $392 for those who were disengaged.[33] Even in industries with high turnover and part-time hourly labor, employee engagement has a positive correlation with reduced turnover, higher store ratings, higher customer satisfaction, and as much as 10% revenue growth.

The case for engaging people at work simply makes sense. Beyond the concrete financial returns of a highly engaged work force, there are also intangible values. The reputation of the company, team spirit, a sense of loyalty, and excitement in the work itself are additional benefits that make a compelling case for engagement.

The question is then, how can leaders unleash their worker's full productive potential? In order to answer this question, I met with groups of highly engaged employees and their managers. Based on engagement survey results and professional experiences, these organization are clearly among the most engaged.

As I met with workers and interviewed managers I asked them what made their groups fully engaged. The answer was not what I was expecting, but the implications are quite simple and profound. Listening to their answers and observing these highly engaged teams at work shows that engagement is not a process or a program. It is not even a practiced behavior resulting from training. Engagement is a contagious positive attitude about our work.

Creating Engaging Conditions

When you walk into fully engaged companies' reception areas or stores, you can immediately tell that something exciting is going on. The buzz is in the air. You can sense the positive energy as people busily go about their work. Everyone seems willing to help you, and you feel instantly welcomed as a guest.

Engagement can't be faked. You cannot, for example, pretend to involve a group of people in an assignment and then not use their input. Managers cannot go around greeting people as if they really cared just to win future favors, or giving praise and recognition to an employee to soften the blow before delivering critical news. People are way too smart for that form of covert manipulation.

Engagement springs from a genuine desire to treat others the way we want to be treated. You've got to feel it! Yet it goes even beyond that as you begin to understand how others prefer to be treated. This requires us to know the people we work with and to understand what makes them tick.

> **Engagement springs from a genuine desire to treat others the way we want to be treated.**

People are engaged by different aspects of the job. Different functions within the same organization are typically engaged by different drivers. Hospital employees, for example, may be bound by the common mission of providing healthcare services to the community. Yet physicians may thrive in an environment that promotes high medical achievement and competitive peer relationships. The nursing staff may respond best by being treated with respect and having the right tools and equipment. Hospital administrators may be energized by opportunities for career advancement and an increased span of responsibilities.

Knowing what to do for each group of people requires sound understanding of what motivates them. Even within the same function, groups may be engaged by different drivers, depending on their industry. Typically, sales representative are motivated by high risk and high reward opportunities, yet they may be engaged differently depending on if they belong to an established pharmaceutical firm or are part of a technology start-up.

Regional differences, the organization's values, and the work force make-up also play a role in determining what engages the people in an organization. In the same city, a local community hospital may engage its workers by promoting a sense of belonging and a noble purpose, while an academic research medical center may engage most effectively by focusing on high achievement and individual freedom.

> **Highly engaged organizations create the conditions where the best people can consistently excel.**

Given the right conditions, every group can be fully engaged. Everyone in the team needs to consider what culture they want to create, and act accordingly. For the manager, it is important to consider what will make each person excel.

Highly engaged organizations create the conditions where their best people can consistently excel. They don't try to be all things to all people. Instead, highly engaged organizations identify what motivates top performers in their culture. Then they provide the conditions that attract and motivate the type of people they seek. By consistently engaging the right people, they achieve peak performance.

Creating a high performing culture is a matter of consistently living up to one's values. An organization's culture is the most accurate reflection of its values. The role of a leader is to institutionalize those values in the organization. They do that by aligning leadership behaviors, training, rewards, and recognition to reinforce those values.

A highly engaged organization will show a dominant driver of engagement that is consistently emphasized. Highly engaged organizations channel their energy and resources in a disciplined way to emphasize core drivers of engagement. These are represented by the five drivers of engagement: High Achievement, Exciting Opportunities, Sense of Belonging, Noble Purpose, and Individual Freedom.

The Five Drivers of Engagement

High
Achievement

**Individual
Freedom**   **Exciting
Opportunities**

Drivers of
Engagement

**Noble
Purpose**   **Sense of
Belonging**

High Achievement

People driven by high achievement seek to reach well-defined goals in a highly competitive environment. High achievers advance by increasing their level of responsibility in the organization or expanding their influence among peers. Preferably high achievers want to grow in both power and respect.

Typical examples of high achievement organizations are banks, law firms, well-established business consulting firms, and research medical centers. These organizations seek to attract people with high qualifications, advanced certifications, and a track record of achievement. They engage top performers through well-paid positions, important titles, advancement opportunities, and a highly competitive environment.

Exciting Opportunities

Individuals engaged by exciting opportunities seek for challenging assignments. They are willing to take risks as long as they can realize high rewards. They thrive in a positive environment where others enthusiastically celebrate success and have fun. People in these organizations pursue ambitious goals, create valuable opportunities, and build energy and enthusiasm.

Typical companies thriving on exciting opportunities are start-ups and entrepreneurial firms, high-technology companies, and sales organizations. These companies seek to attract people who are willing to take substantial risks, create new opportunities, and build a culture of success. Exciting opportunities organizations engage people with virtually unlimited rewards that are directly proportional to their contribution. They celebrate value creation with enthusiasm and, based on the amount of risk, may provide ownership incentives in the enterprise.

Sense of Belonging

A sense of belonging motivates people seeking for a dependable job that provides a stable income and benefits. They want to be treated with dignity and respect and value a supportive working environment where they can establish cooperative relationships. Their contributions are integrating diverse views and inputs to implement reliable processes.

Manufacturing companies, such as steel production, aviation or automotive manufacturing, government organizations, and the armed forces exemplify sense of belonging. These organizations engage their people by fostering a family-like culture in which long-term players are valued for their dedication and adherence to performance standards. They recognize employees for developing formal processes, policies, and standards that enable people to contribute over time.

Noble Purpose

Contributing to a noble cause is paramount to people who have strong group values, are willing to render acts of service, and make sacrifices in fulfilling a duty. They exhibit visible pride in the organization's reputation and foster loyalty and camaraderie among its members.

Special security operations like the police or the Coast Guard, scientific groups like NASA or the American Cancer Society, and faith-based organizations like churches or humanitarian services groups engage their members by evoking a noble purpose. These organizations provide a sustained level of commitment to their members. These organizations infuse their noble purpose through values-based leadership, a rich history of distinguished reputation, and visible external and internal recognition.

Individual Freedom

Individual freedom is a primary driver of engagement for people seeking flexible work schedules, personal growth opportunities, and respected peer association. For these individuals, the organization is simply a vehicle to facilitate their unique contribution. These individuals prefer to work with a great deal of autonomy to do specialized work, develop core competencies, and build a peer network.

Typical organizations in which individual freedom is a primary driver of engagement are construction companies that rely on contractors, healthcare management organizations that administer a network of independent physicians, and academic research colleges that employ prestigious faculty. The relationship between the workers and the organization is based on contracts, credentials, and skill levels. These organizations engage top talent by providing them flexible work schedules, incentives for advanced certifications, and access to a reputable network.

The chart below provides a summary of the needs and wants of the individual and the engagement levers for the organization. High engagement happens when both conditions are met—when the needs and wants of both the enterprise and the employees are satisfied. Leaders who identify these common interests actively use the levers of engagement to bring value for both parties.

Making Engagement Work

Drivers of Engagement	Needs & Wants of the Individual	Engagement Levers for the Organization
High Achievement	• Opportunities for advancement • Clear performance measures • Control over resources • Provide task focus	1. Substantial rewards for goal achievement 2. Titles and reporting relationships 3. Control over budgets and resources 4. Opportunities for promotion 5. Competitive peer relationships
Exciting Opportunities	• Challenging assignments • High reward opportunities • To celebrate and have fun • Create value	1. Virtually unlimited financial upside 2. Entrepreneurial incentives 3. Achieve challenging assignments 4. Enthusiastic celebration of contributions 5. Fun and energizing environment
Sense of Belonging	• Dependable income and benefits • Be treated with dignity and respect • Supportive worker relationships • Integrate and reconcile inputs	1. Consistent compensation and benefits 2. The right tools and equipment 3. Peer collaboration and respect 4. Organize resources and set processes 5. Recognition of tenure and dedication
Noble Purpose	• A noble cause • Strong group values • Pride in the group reputation • Render acts of service	1. Sustained provision of resources 2. A rich history and noble mission 3. Value driven leadership 4. Important group assignments 5. Visible external and internal recognition
Individual Freedom	• Autonomy to do the job • Personal growth opportunities • Respected peer association • Perform specialized work	1. Pay based on contracts and credentials 2. Flexible work schedules 3. Supervisor available when needed 4. Incentives for advanced certifications 5. Access to a respected peer network

The five drivers of engagement describe five distinct approaches to motivating people. Organizations, like individuals, display a preference for one of the key drivers. Emphasizing the primary driver yields the highest performance gains for the employee and for the enterprise. Most organizations, however, use more than one of the key drivers to engage employees. The balance of the five drivers within a company create a unique engagement profile.

Understanding an organization's engagement profile provides insights for motivating its members. Teams realize the greatest value from their members by leveraging their unique engagement drivers and emphasizing those drivers that align with the team engagement profile and deemphasizing those that are least preferred. Team members receive the most value from their work when their actions are reinforced by the team's drivers.

Changing the attitude and behavior of thousands of people is very, very hard to accomplish. You can't simply give a couple of speeches or write a new credo for the company and declare that a new culture has taken hold. You can't mandate it, can't engineer it. What you can do is create the conditions for transformation.

~Lou Gerstner

Leading High Performing Teams

Unable to secure a high-paying summer job selling pesticides door-to-door in California, Todd Peterson decided instead to cut a deal with the manufacturer and sell the products directly. Peterson took a dozen friends along with him and little else besides their sleeping bags and plenty of motivation as they set out to sell. Living in a trailer at a relative's horse-breeding ranch, working long hours, and borrowing money to buy the product, Peterson figured out what it took to succeed in that business. By the end of the summer the group of students had managed to make enough money to pay for their next year's tuition, living expenses, and much more.

Over the following 15 years, Peterson continued refining the business model, eventually becoming the CEO of APX Alarm Security Solutions, the second largest and fastest growing home security provider in North America. APX currently creates over

1,000 high-income job opportunities for college students every summer.

In APX's corporate offices, one immediately notices the entrepreneurial energy driving the enterprise. Young people wearing jeans, T-shirts, and baseball caps pace about the corporate open spaces gathering for meetings, discussing sales figures over their laptops, and communicating via handheld devices. Make no mistake about these youthful characters. These are not just entry-level workers; many of them are sales managers and other senior officers who are gearing up for the action-packed summer months.

Posters on the walls and fliers lying around everywhere announce all kinds of sales contests, employee celebrations, and charitable events. There's always a reason to celebrate something at APX Alarm. In all cases the substantial awards are directly tied to outstanding sales performance. Pool tables and workout facilities complement the APX Alarm work culture. It is common to find sales representatives and top executives talking business while doing a workout during work hours.

The company is also actively involved in serving the local community and making contributions to international humanitarian aid, an altruistic balance to their pragmatic focus on making money. At APX Alarm, making huge amounts of money and serving the world's less fortunate are inextricably connected.

In order to understand what it takes to be fully engaged at APX Alarm, I met with the 2008 best-selling representative, Mark Bench. Over the last four summers, by working only four months, Bench has managed to double his income every year, now reaching well over $300,000. Not bad for a guy in his 20s putting himself through school! His success is no accident; Mark prepares for the rigor of his summer job with the focus and determination of an elite athlete.

During the off months, Bench carefully selects the people for his sales team. Recruiting talent above his own, says Bench, is a key to reaching his full potential. He recruits only those who see the opportunity and are highly motivated to work with him. "I prefer a few solid quality people rather than a large team,"

says Bench. Then he takes the time to train his team and prepare them well ahead of the starting date. "We listen to real
sales pitches, get excited about doing them, and role-play sales
approaches over and over. We want to practice every objection
and refine our response."

In anticipation of the summer months, Bench analyzes his
past performance by going over the previous year's sales records.
He adjusts his plans based on past experiences. He also reads
business books to glean practical principles that will enhance
his sales strategy.

When he is finally in the field selling, Bench finds ways to
keep himself and his team totally focused hour after hour, day
after day, for the duration of the four summer months. It helps
maximize performance to set specific goals for short durations of
time, says Bench. He sets personal contests with his teammates
for the best performance in a given morning, and then raising
the stakes for the best results by the end of the day. As the weeks
go on, the need to stay highly focused increases, so Bench comes
up with new and exciting ideas to celebrate success.

Bench wastes no time managing others' performance. "In a
high performing sales team there is no need for managing others. I notice that when I do well, my team does well," says Bench.
"So I constantly ask myself: what can *I* do better?" He notices
that this self-improvement attitude permeates the team, so
everyone starts focusing on doing their best. At the end of every
day Bench checks his performance against the top 10 representatives for the entire company. As a team, they analyze their
statistics and watch video interviews of top performers posted
on the company's website. Not surprisingly, Bench and his team
are often featured.

"At the end of the day, making money is not enough of an
incentive to keep us going like this for four months," says Bench
as he reflects on what kept him and his team going. "We need a
higher goal to keep us motivated. Our focus is to become the best-
selling team in the world. Nothing short of an extremely exciting goal can keep us working so hard for so long." While Bench
and his team work diligently toward becoming the best-selling

team in the world, APX Alarm provides the exciting opportunities they and others like them need to reach their full potential.

Nothing is so infectious as example.

~Francois de la Rochefocauld

While exciting opportunities and high achievement keep a sales team reaching for top performance, hourly restaurant workers are engaged by very different drivers. El Pollo Loco, a fast-growing restaurant chain that specializes in flame-grilled chicken, has been spreading from its birthplace in Southern California across the United States. Operating more than 400 restaurants, El Pollo Loco serves fresh Mexican-inspired entrees with its signature citrus-marinated grilled chicken. What keeps over 3,000 El Pollo Loco restaurant employees sizzling about their work?

Restaurant employees at El Pollo Loco rave about their food! The highest engagement score for restaurant employees is about the quality of their food. "We serve the best chicken in town!" affirms one of the restaurant workers with visible pride. "The food is great, I love to eat here," comments another restaurant worker. Stephen Carley, president and CEO of El Pollo Loco is well aware of the importance of serving consistently fresh, perfectly flame-broiled, and flavorful chicken.

Besides the sense of pride in the quality of food they serve, El Pollo Loco restaurant crews are engaged by their relationship with their manager. The working conditions are what make El Pollo Loco attractive to the hourly employees. Restaurant managers are constantly trained and reminded of their role in creating the right conditions for their crew. When managers set clear expectations, treat employees with respect, and provide a clean and safe working environment, employees thrive.

Artemio Pureco has been a restaurant manager at El Pollo Loco since 2001, regularly turning troubled units into high-performing restaurants. His restaurants have consistently received the highest employee engagement scores. His approach for managing high-turnover hourly workers is simple and effective.

When he starts an assignment at a new restaurant, Pureco first observes the people at work. He gets to know each person and talks with them as a genuine friend. But for Pureco, strong relationships don't conflict with running a good business.

After a few weeks of close observation, Pureco picks the good ones and lets the poor performers go. "I get rid of the people who can't or won't do an excellent job," states Pureco confidently. "I tell them as I come in. I need the right people on board to make the restaurant work. If we can make the place successful, everyone wins."

Even as he lets go of poor performers, Pureco maintains a friendly and respectful demeanor, which is much appreciated by the crew. Then, as he brings in new people, he makes sure that the new employees feel welcomed by everybody and that they all work as a team. "Nobody's job is more important than another's. We are all important!" he says.

"They are all like my family," he candidly admits. To create a supportive working environment, Pureco goes beyond strictly business, as he talks with all employees as equals. "I treat them like my best friends. I am confident that if they leave it is only because they have a much better job, or because they haven't done a good job. But they always leave as friends. Even those I have fired come back and visit me."

The employees are quick to acknowledge that Pureco does not exaggerate when describing the genuine care he feels for each crew member. The employees say that they can ask Pureco for advice and he is always willing to listen and help. He works alongside the crew to train them to become future managers. Several of his former employees are now managing their own restaurants.

Pureco knows that some employees need certain working hours and days off to meet personal needs. He accommodates those needs, even if it takes longer to do the schedule. "As long as we can make it work, I give them the hours and days off they need." He noticed that this level of commitment pays off in many ways. "I always take care of my people and they take care of me," says Pureco. "That is how we consistently pass inspection and get 100% ratings on cleanliness and safety."

When it comes to performance, Pureco makes no compromises. "We can't let performance down because we are friends. If some people are having personal problems that are affecting their work performance, I tell them they now have another problem: They can't work with me. There are no hard feelings. They know I only work with top performing people."

Customers also find themselves among friends at the restaurant. Pureco talks openly about treating customers as friends. "We want to learn their names, know their favorite items, and make them feel comfortable. We want them to enjoy the food and have a good time. That's how we run a high-value store and are always beating last year's sales."

Working at El Pollo Loco with managers like Artemio Pureco, employees find just what they want. For them, a great job means a reliable income, a supportive work environment, and a sense of pride in what they do. To them, their manager is the face and heart of the company. As the restaurant manager does his or her best to provide a genuine sense of belonging, the employees in return do their best to deliver delicious, quality food and excellent customer service.

Considering the engagement profile of different high-performing teams, we can conclude that there is no single list of attributes that engages every group of people. Understanding what engages a group of people unlocks the secret to achieving high performance. Managers who make the most of their people consistently apply the drivers of engagement.

Coaching for High Performance

The role of the supervisor is critical for turning an average team into one that consistently performs at a higher performance level. Unfortunately, most managers don't know how to make the most of their people. They ask, "How do I motivate the people in my team?" Essentially, they want to know what they can do to help specific individuals do a better job. The leader's personal example coupled with appropriate coaching is what helps improve others' performance.

The most powerful form of influence is personal example. After all, we are the only person we can really change. By changing ourselves, we can change how others respond to us. To be a leader is to model a way for others to follow.

There is, however, more we can do beyond being a good example. We facilitate change for others through coaching. Coaching is an ongoing development process that provides feedback, supports growth, and challenges employees to do better. The objective of coaching is to build a stronger relationship of trust with the person being coached.

> # By changing ourselves, we can change how others respond to us.

Most of us don't think of ourselves as being a coach, mainly because it is not our job title or part of our job description. Hence, we go about our busy day without paying attention to coaching opportunities. A person we work with or an employee we supervise may need assistance. If we do happen to notice the need, we tend to jump in and quickly solve the problem. "Do this!" "Try that." "You need to . . . ." We prefer to tell others what to do. When we do that, however, we instantly lose a coaching opportunity.

The most influential leaders look for coaching opportunities. They know that they are more powerful when they allow others to come up with solutions. As they exercise the art of persuasion, they help others commit to a course of action rather than merely comply with a command. As a result of coaching, others learn faster, deliver higher quality, and produce greater value.

In the next coaching opportunity that comes along, notice how you approach the situation. If you didn't get the best possible outcome, how else would you like others to respond? Your approach determines how others act and what results you will get.

It is true that some situations require a more direct approach. Telling others what to do is most appropriate when others are seeking guidance, such as when people are new on the job, the task is routine and simple, or strict compliance is required. Other situations that require precise directions can be determined by risk and timing, including cases where you need immediate results or when there are severe consequences for failure.

All other situations, where people are acting responsibly, require a less direct approach. For example, when dealing with an experienced worker or when the task is part of a broader responsibility or when the task requires judgment, it is better to invest additional time for coaching.

The most appropriate coaching approach depends on the situation. If we are dealing with blatantly bad behavior or unacceptable performance, we must set clear standards and enforce discipline consistently. However, if we want to enhance adequate conduct or improve what is already working well, we need to gain buy-in and enlist commitment. We cannot force a person who is already doing a good job into doing a better one. In order to reach peak performance, the coach facilitates others to direct their growth.

Let's start with the most challenging case of coaching: someone who is not meeting minimal job expectations. The person refuses to take responsibility for his actions. Whenever you point out a problem, he responds with retorts such as, "It's not my job!" "Others do it too." "Well, just tell me what you want me to do." Such replies deflect responsibility. There are entrenched reasons why the person is acting irresponsibly at the risk of his employment.

Spending lots of time trying to reason with this person's behavior is futile. Worse yet, getting into an argument will prove counterproductive. In this case, an effective coach simply describes the specific problem behavior and its consequences to the person. While doing this it is important to remain calm, clear, and matter-of-fact about the case. The person must feel that he is being treated with respect, as a responsible and competent individual. The coach concludes the conversation by asking for a commitment to more acceptable conduct in the future.

Attempting to justify a softer approach, some people say, "I'm just too nice." They are missing the point. Administering discipline never equates with being mean. In fact, the approach doesn't work unless one is nice. In becoming nasty, one descends to a lower level and loses the influential power of example. What is required of us in such situations is to be firm and consistent. An effective coach is both firm *and* nice with people at all times.

To help a person whose conduct is acceptable but could be better requires an entirely different approach that builds on his or her own ideas for improvement. Coaching starts by helping the person identify a specific goal or desired outcome. The coach then helps the other person realize the gap between the current and the desired situation. Once the need for change is clear, the coach asks probing questions to help the other person discover possible solutions. Effective coaching allows the person to explore his or her options and choose a course of action.

An effective coach helps others learn how to solve their own problems. The exchange builds confidence in the individual's capacity to reach goals, anticipate challenges, and take the necessary steps forward. The coach does not need to be a subject matter expert to help those individuals improve who know what they are doing.

How, for example, would you go about coaching Tiger Woods in the game of golf? He already knows far more about the game than most others. Even elite players may not have much advice for someone at that level. Coaching a top performer who is making a superior contribution may seem intimidating. Yet coaching a person who is on top of their game is the most valuable and rewarding experience.

Reaching peak performance builds on the drivers of engagement. At this point, the need for managing evaporates. There is no need for supervision when people take full responsibility for their own performance. The role of the leader is simply to create the conditions for engagement in which others can thrive. The leader of a high-performing team acts as a coach to bring out the best in others, remove performance barriers, and facilitate goal achievement. By inspiring teamwork and collaboration, the leader engages ordinary people in doing extraordinary work.

Given the right circumstances, quite ordinary
people consistently do extraordinary things.

~ Dee Hock, founder of VISA

Putting Others' Needs First

When leading change one would expect some level of resistance. Invariably, not everyone will be onboard; some will disagree with decisions and others will find ways to stall implementation. During a downturn, resistance to change increases as people feel insecure about their jobs. Ironically, it is precisely during challenging times when companies need most to engage their workforce.

Failure to inspire teamwork and collaboration in a time of crisis devastates a company's capacity to change. In the greatest change failures, leaders dealt forcefully with resistance, reasoning that they had to make tough choices that employees would not like. Consequently, employees became divided and the change was compromised.

In the most successful transformations, however, leaders and employees banded together. Leaders talked openly with their employees about what was at stake. Together they found ways to cooperate and often made voluntary sacrifices for the common good. Leaders had to earn the trust of their employees in working together for a common cause. Finding what others want has been vividly illustrated in a story attributed to Ralph Waldo Emerson.

In the ranch, there was always too much to do. From sun up to sun down the men labored diligently all the hot summer long. From mending fences, to digging ditches, to feeding cattle, or looking for a stray animal—the job was never done. That's why no one had much patience when it came to getting a stubborn calf back in the barn after a long day of work.

Ralph, one of the seasoned lead hands, asked Jimmy for help. They had to get one calf into the barn before he got sick from overeating. The two men went after the calf on their horses, followed by their herding dog. Typically, that would do it even for a lazy cow, but this calf had just lost his mother and was unyielding.

No amount of men yelling or dogs barking at the tender calf would move him. When the horsemen charged really close to him, he would barely move a few steps and then would stop again. The sullen look in the calf eyes defied the trio as if saying, "You can't make me do anything. No matter what you do, I just don't care."

As other ranch hands finished their duties, they lined up by the barn to see the show. "I bet you Ralph will get that calf into the barn even if he has to carry it up," said one of the spectators to a fellow worker. But the more tricks they tried on the poor calf, the more he rebelled.

Hot, tired, and dusty, Ralph was ready to get tough on the calf. He got the rope and the shovel. While all the ranch hands now sat under the shade of a large tree watching, Ralph instructed Jimmy carefully, "He needs to go in, so I'll push him with the stick and you'll pull him with the rope."

The calf saw both men approaching him, tools in hand with a fierce, tired look. Paralyzed with fear, he stiffened his legs and stubbornly refused to leave the pasture. The struggle intensified. Ralph started swearing at the beast while Jimmy was pulling from his horse and the dog was barking incessantly—and they were all enveloped in a cloud of dust.

The Irish housemaid saw their predicament. She knew instinctively what the calf wanted, so she walked to the fearful calf and put her thick finger in the calf's mouth and let the calf suck at her finger as she gently led him into the barn.[34]

There is no such a thing as resistance to change. There is only resistance to pain. Whether you are dealing with people or with calves, it is important to remember what the other wants. The cowboys were thinking only of what they wanted—even if that wasn't what was best for the animal. The calf, likewise, was doing just what he wanted.

In the end, nobody can force even a good thing on anyone else, let alone a bad thing! The housemaid thought of what the calf wanted and succeeded where the cowboys had failed. Give people what they want and they may come a long way to give you what you want as well. When we think of the other person first, we can earn their support. For individuals and teams, achieving full engagement is a form of love.

Love is the condition in which the happiness of another person is essential to your own.

~Robert Heinlein

Chapter Review

Summary

An organization can reach its full potential when the members are fully engaged. Creating the conditions for engagement requires understanding what attracts and motivates the best people. It may take time to cultivate an engaging culture, especially if leaders have to overcome a history of low trust or weak commitment. The best way to start is by example, inspiring teamwork and commitment through one's actions. Coaching for high performance is another way to inspire others to reach their full potential. For a leader this means addressing poor performance firmly and consistently, while facilitating a learning process so everyone can excel.

Key Points

* To achieve peak performance, people need to be fully engaged.
* Engagement is the voluntary dedication to doing one's best work.
* People become fully engaged when they commit to a cause.
* Engagement is a benefit to the employee and the organization.
* People are engaged by different drivers.
* Organizations can create the conditions where the best people can consistently excel.

Group Discussion

1. How engaged are the members of our team?
2. What attracts the best people to our team?
3. What motivates peak performance in our team?
4. How do we create the conditions in which the best people consistently excel?
5. How can we increase teamwork and commitment?

Access additional Ascent Tools at
www.ascent-advisor.com/tools.html

The Ascent Process
5Es for Mastering Change

Build Common Purpose	Clarify Direction	Develop Capacity	Inspire Commitment	**Achieve Results**
Envision	Evaluate	Empower	Engage	**Evolve**
What do we want to see happen?	How can we make it happen?	How do we build on strengths?	How do we inspire collaboration?	**How do we track progress?**

## CHAPTER EIGHT

Achieve Results

Evolve: How do we track progress?

Excellent firms don't believe in excellence—
only in constant improvement and constant change.

~Tom Peters

Getting Amazing Results

Since the invention of the integrated circuit in 1958, computing power has increased exponentially, doubling approximately every two years. The trend was first observed by Intel co-founder Gordon E. Moore, and has continued to accelerate for almost half a century.[†] Moore's Law, as it has become known, represents not just a technological breakthrough, but also an organizational one.

Coming up with an innovative microprocessor design that not just improves, but *doubles* the processing power of the fastest chip in the market, is an amazing engineering feat. But, coming up with a company that orchestrates such breakthroughs

---

† Although originally calculated as a doubling every year, Moore later refined the period to two years. It is often incorrectly quoted as a doubling of transistors every 18 months, as David House, an Intel Executive, gave that period to chip performance increase. The actual period was about 20 months.[35]

consistently every two years, is pure leadership genius. Intel is one of the Change Masters that has done just that.

Looking inside Intel, one can find a simple concept driving the complex organizational circuitry: discipline. Intel faced rivals in multiple market niches, each pursuing strategies similar to Intel's. Motorola, IBM, Apple, AMD, Toshiba, and Hitachi, just to name a few, competed in the computer chip industry. Intel combated them by simply being the best, systematically perfecting every aspect of the business, from design to service.

Andy Grove knew that in order to eliminate the ever-increasing competition, Intel had to consistently do one thing—microprocessors—better than anyone else. To achieve that goal, Grove asked his managers to push the envelope in every direction. Managers received wide latitude to experiment and be innovative, but they had to measure their performance every step of the way. From the design of microprocessors to the marketing campaigns to the way they conducted management meetings, Grove insisted on constant improvement.[36]

Grove engineered an organization capable of producing a continuous flow of radical innovation. The complex designs that account for the speed of Intel's chip went through a competitive process that was far fiercer than the competitors'. Intel set up competing engineering teams to vie for the next breakthrough. The teams with the most talented ideas received additional resources. Less promising designs were disbanded and reassigned into the winning teams. Through a rigorous elimination process, only the best designs succeeded. Yet, long before the winning chip was proclaimed as the best in market, Intel engineering teams were already working on its successor.

In manufacturing, Grove pushed operational capacity beyond foreseeable needs. To excel in manufacturing, Intel invested millions of dollars in plants that could crank out more processors in a day than some rivals did in an entire year. Through precision and automation, Intel's chips became not only the fastest, but also the cheapest to produce.

Furthermore, Grove insisted that his managers measured every aspect of their performance. They were given latitude to experiment and try new things, as long as they were able to learn from their experiences. In order to integrate innovation and discipline, Grove indicated the need for precise measurement and analysis to avoid ambiguity and discover insightful correlations. At one point, after concluding a lengthy and rather unproductive meeting, Grove requested a plan for making future meetings more efficient.

> ## Precise measurement and constant analysis are key to continuous improvement.

Precise measurement and analysis are at the heart of continuous improvement. When dealing in generalities one can only hope to succeed. In fact, without measures, we won't even know if we are succeeding. When we focus on specifics, we cannot fail to improve. Performance measures direct our actions closer to the desired results.

In God we trust, all others bring data.

~W. Edwards Deming

Tracking Performance Indicators

Key indicators measure what matters most in order to achieve results. Rather than tracking every variable that affects performance, key indicators focus on the 20% that impacts 80% of the outcome. The concept is simple, but identifying key indicators requires an in-depth understanding of the cause-and-effect relationship between actions and outcomes.

The dilemma for the workers at the Crown Packaging Burnaby Mill was a choice between shutting down the money-losing operation and losing their source of income, or setting themselves an impossible production goal. From the most seasoned machine operators to the brightest engineer, everyone at the mill agreed that the problem was the machine. The massive equipment that turned sawdust pulp into large rolls of paper was simply too old—inefficient and uncompetitive. It would require large sums of money to fix. But, since no money was available at the time, they were stuck with the old machine.

As a last resort, they called in a retired industry veteran to consult with them about the situation. On his first day on the job, this consultant asked to be taken right to the production area. He skipped meeting the management altogether. He went right to chatting with the machine operators, getting acquainted with them and asking questions. Then, he sat in the middle of the production floor with a notepad in hand, just observing. Occasionally, he would go to an area to watch up close what people were doing, ask a few more questions, and then go back to his observation point.

The first day passed with no new insight. On the second day he did the same; day three, likewise. He observed, walked around, chatted with the workers, and asked an occasional question, but he never told the operator what to do; he only asked why the operator did things certain ways. At times, they would engage in a rather philosophical line of questioning, going deeper into more *why*s about the production process. The entire week went by the same way.

By Friday, workers were voluntarily trying new approaches. They began experimenting with ways to make the line run faster, make the pulp feed more even, and modify the temperatures of the several dryers. Some attempts made things worse; others showed some improvement. Not once during the first five days was there a breakthrough. Instead, each day brought a stimulating slew of trial-and-error approaches that infused the workers with curiosity.

Minor improvements began to add up. Subtle variations would suddenly show big gains down the line. The operators began to isolate and optimize those measures. They were discovering the key performance indicators. Suddenly, there was hope for the old paper mill. Before the end of the week, the line was close to reaching the production and quality targets. Over the next several months, the paper mill's productivity and quality charts showed a pronounced s-curve indicative of its growth.

What actually changed at the old Burnaby paper mill? Certainly the machine was still the same antiquated piece of equipment. The workers were the same crew that had manned the operation for decades, with the same skills and experience. The only difference was their renewed understanding of subtle, yet vital performance indicators. Their productive capacity had always been there; now they knew how to achieve it.

Engineering captured the operators' learning in a fish-bone diagram. The chart showed with connecting lines the cause-and-effect impact of key performance measures. The chart allowed workers to clarify and test their assumptions so that the cause for high productivity was well understood. What the chart could not show was the learning, inquisitive spirit that had changed the minds of the long-time mill workers.

Once we understand how specific performance indicators affect outcomes, we are able to improve results consistently. This takes keen observation and trial-and-error experimentation, because key indicators are not always obvious. Some key indicators require probing and digging to discover the root causes behind apparently unreachable results. In diving deeper to find the key indicators, Toyota employees are trained to ask "why" not once, but five times before settling on the root cause.

Without this level of understanding, we may easily fall prey to the folly of hoping for X while stubbornly measuring Y. Often we measure effort, while hoping for results. We even become frustrated when we can't improve the outcome by increasing our effort. Instead, we need to track what actually produces the desired results. At work as in other areas of life, what we measure is what we get. By changing what we measure, we change what we get.

A goal is a dream with a deadline.

~Napoleon Hill

Holding Each Other Accountable

Accountability consists of making and keeping promises. When we say we will do something, our word becomes our bond for action. No further assurance, in writing or otherwise, should surpass the binding power of the stated commitment. Holding each other accountable starts by confirming the agreement, clarifying mutual responsibilities, and following through on progress.

These simple steps are all too often ignored, by one or both sides. If we fall short of fulfilling a commitment, we make up excuses. Conditions change, things become more difficult, or we just get too busy with other priorities. Whatever the excuse, when we do this we erode trust in a relationship, a team, an organization, and society.

Such was the case when Steve, one of my clients, received feedback from his peers. Steve was shocked when he saw that his direct reports rated him low in integrity. Lower, in fact, than the company norm. "How could it be?" he asked incredulously. "I know I am honest. I tell the truth. I haven't done anything unethical. This report is just not valid. They are upset with me, and they are taking it out in the assessment."

I explained to Steve that low scores in integrity usually reflect failure to follow through on promises. Steve was pensive. "Could that be it?" he mused while reflecting on his team's last strategic retreat.

The promising strategic event held everyone's expectations for addressing frustrating issues affecting the entire team. Steve specifically asked his team leaders to prepare for the offsite meeting, and they spent much time and energy coming up with ideas and recommendations. Everyone knew the meeting was going to be a hit.

They couldn't have been more mistaken. Steve's priorities dominated the agenda. The team leaders soon realized that little or no time was left to discuss their ideas. Besides, nobody wanted to spoil the comfortable ambiance and enjoyable social interaction at the event by bringing up critical issues. So the strategic offsite became a fun time with polite interaction.

Steve later admitted that his idea for the offsite meeting was more about having a good time. Taking the time away from the office for thinking outside of the box was for Steve more important than solving actual problems. At the retreat, Steve laid out 12 strategic projects for the coming year. The team concealed their surprise at the long list of strategic priorities and added some of their own ideas. Steve's team came back to their jobs, renewed by the enjoyable time away from the office and ready to move forward.

Then Steve and his team got busy. A week later, Steve's assistant sent the participants an email summarizing the strategic goals. Two weeks later, Steve held a meeting to review the goals. Five weeks later the items remained unassigned and unresolved.

Two months later, the team was still doing the same things they had always done. The strategy continued essentially unchanged. The goals were soon conveniently forgotten. More importantly, the team lost their excitement. One of the old timers expressed her bitter disappointment: "That's what we always do, we get excited, we come up with ideas, we make big plans, and then nothing really happens. If Steve is not following through, why should we?"

Holding one's self accountable is essential to getting others to do anything. The role of the leader is not an easy one in this respect, as all eyes are on the leader's actions. Ambitious plans are easier made than carried out. How leaders delegate assignments, follow through, and give feedback on performance can either set the organization in motion or bring it to a standstill.

The Steps to Accountability model helps teams clarify mutual commitments in a productive way. It is the role of the leader to delegate assignments, set deadlines, and follow up on progress. It is, however, a reciprocal responsibility to make good on those agreements. Both parties have to help each other understand, accept, and maintain their end of the commitment. This is best done by describing the commitment, confirming agreement, and following up through regular feedback and reporting. Making and keeping commitments builds our capacity to achieve increasingly higher goals.

Steps to Accountability

COMMITMENT
Describe the specific commitment
each person is making.

AGREEMENT
Confirm mutual agreement on
the rights and responsibilities.

FOLLOW UP
Setup frequent progress
feedback and reporting.

Steve realized that poor delegation and lack of follow-through
were behind his low integrity scores. He asked for coaching to
assist him in regaining the trust of his team members. Steve recognized that asking people to prepare input and then to not give
them the time to present their ideas backfired. Moreover, having
him set all the priorities made everything dependent on Steve.
Others were reluctant to take responsibility without the necessary authority to act. There was little buy-in since everyone was
working exclusively on Steve's goals.

These challenges are the cause behind a team's failure to
deliver results. The common mistake is when leaders focus solely
on holding others accountable, as if the problem is not theirs.
They clarify expectations, expecting others to follow through
without checking on their end of the agreement. The remedy is
to hold each other mutually accountable.

When accountability is a two-way street, both parties want
to understand what they can do to facilitate the other's performance. Assignments are not just orders, but reflect a mutual
agreement between both parties. Authority is given with the

responsibility to carry out the assignments, thus increasing commitment. Confidence grows as regular feedback and reporting keeps everyone informed of progress. Follow-through reaffirms the initial commitment and builds trust in the relationship.

Take a quick inventory of your team's current level of accountability. Is your team consistently achieving its goals? Are people delivering what they have promised on time? After a meeting, does everyone have a clear understanding of what was agreed on during the meeting? Are you reporting regularly on key performance measures? If you recognize a need for improvement in any of these areas, start by asking yourself what you can do to increase mutual accountability.

It is no use saying "we are doing our best."
You have to succeed in doing what is necessary.

~Winston Churchill

Reviewing Progress Milestones

Picture this casual hallway conversation between a chief financial officer and one of his subordinates:

"By the way, how's the team working on Accounts Payable doing?" asks the CFO, curiously.

"The AP team is doing well. They are off to a good start. They have a great attitude. They are still on the planning stages, which may take some time to finalize, but what a great opportunity it is to have them onboard!"

Translation: The project is in real trouble. If it doesn't show some results quickly, it may be scrapped. Compare the first response with the following:

"The AP project? Let me tell you, in the first 30 days they have reduced accounts payable from 62 to 59 days. They have a goal to get us to collect in 45 days. That's just the beginning, this month they are . . . ."

Translation: The AP project is a total success. What they are doing is working, and it is likely to expand in scope.

What's the difference? Results!

Initial conditions set the pattern in motion. The Change Masters delivered results from the start. At these companies, a new pattern in management decisions was instantly clear to the employees. The positive shift was soon picked up by the press, which started to report encouraging news about these companies. Customers began noticing improved products and services from these companies, making them more attractive. Word spread quickly and within months, the outcomes of a change became increasingly more visible.

When an initiative fails to produce positive results within a relatively short time, it is likely to fail in the long-run. The Change Failures all started ambitious transformations, often with great fanfare and high expectations. Results were projected to come, soon enough they thought, after sufficient planning and thorough analysis and political considerations and much more. The implementation process stalled and results were never completely realized.

> **Initial results indicate how an initiative is likely to continue over time.**

To set our sights on the right target, we need to focus on results, not activities. Defining a change as a strategic alignment, a reorganization, a cultural transformation, or a process reengineering is focusing on the activity. Many such activities fail to deliver the anticipated results simply because that is what they were intended to be from the start—an activity!

A change that starts with results in mind is defined in terms of reducing costs, increasing revenues, improving quality, expanding markets, increasing productivity, or creating new offerings. These are all terms that denote concrete business outcomes. As long as the change process starts and stays with results, we are far more likely to achieve real objectives.

Results need to remain the constant of the initiative. It is easy for managers and consultants to mistake the means for the ends. The tools, processes, or methodologies used to achieve a result consume so much attention that they may displace focus on the actual goal. How one achieves a result is important, but it is of secondary importance to the actual result.

Achieving results early is critical to gaining credibility and making the rest of the change viable. Aiming for early wins helps everyone stay focused on results. Successful change targets gains that can be achieved in the near term. One may need to overinvest resources upfront to ensure that early wins are fully achieved, beyond what anyone thought possible. Then, the clear evidence of initial success keeps the center of attention where it should be—on results!

The concept of early wins can be difficult for some to grasp. Some people would point out that given the nature of their project, it would take up to 12 to 18 months to deliver anything meaningful. They make the case that they need time and investment *before* they can deliver results. It is true that most significant accomplishments do require time and resources to complete. But that doesn't exclude the need to show tangible progress toward the long-term goals.

Early wins need to be legitimate victories. This is not the result of a contrived accounting miracle to make the numbers look good. Some companies get used to moving around revenue and costs numbers to make their reports more acceptable. Instead of solving the real problems, they edit the reports. Such murky practice distorts the truth, confuses future decisions, and perpetrates errors. Moreover, this practice is dangerously addictive as it usually requires additional cover ups verging on illegal accounting. Early wins need to reflect real results.

A results-oriented project sets specific milestones for continuing to achieve results overtime. Progress toward milestones can be assessed at regular intervals through progress review meetings. Milestones serve as check points to verify progress, evaluate conditions, and make course corrections.

Milestones provide the opportunity to evaluate current results and make the necessary adjustments. Anticipating milestones allows us to be accountable for results as we compare how we are doing against our goal. It is far more credible to say, "We saved

$50,000 last month against a goal of $150,000," than to say, "We experienced typical project startup issues, but we remain fully committed to saving $2,000,000 by the end of the year."

Progress reviews are an excellent forum for reviewing milestones and making strategic adjustments. Forget about the formal strategic planning meetings with the hefty binders full of numbers! What we want is a dynamic discussion with solid debate, open dialogue, and personal ownership of business goals. Team members attending progress reviews need to come ready to bring up observations, exchange ideas, and speak their minds. One way to facilitate this is to have participants gather information in advance and come prepared with an update to report at the progress reviews.

Accounts of progress reviews at the Change Masters differ widely from what was happening at the Change Failures. A person sitting at a leadership meeting with each of these two groups of companies would immediately notice a huge difference. At the 10 most successful changes, leaders did not use the formal corporate strategic planning process. Instead, they involved their key players in a dynamic exchange of ideas and actions.

At General Electric, for example, Jack Welch immediately dispensed with the PowerPoint slide presentations and the fat financial books they had traditionally used at strategic planning meetings. He replaced those with a dynamic and real exchange, which went on for nearly four hours, and during which Welch listened, lectured, coaxed, and queried his leaders. The managers pushed right back, too, often challenging assumptions, expressing ideas, and calling out the inconsistencies.

A GE executive complained that despite the rhetoric about managing for the long term, they were under too much pressure to produce short-term results. Others joined in support, pointing out that the company's relentless push for top of industry results, the most aggressive initiative of the kind ever mounted in corporate America, had caused intense internal competition, resulting in lost opportunities to learn and sell services across the vast network of GE companies.

Pacing the floor with a bottle of water in hand, Welch responded, "I don't mind a little competition as long as we get the results. If it bothers you, stop it! Find ways to get results and collaborate if you prefer." Going back to the first point, Welch looked straight at the person who made the comment and stated flatly, "You can't grow long term if you can't eat short term." He looked around the group and added, "Anybody can manage short. Anybody can manage long. Balancing those two things is what management is." Hearts pounded, heads turned, leaders went out of the meeting knowing they had a shot to operate with one of the best companies, and the rest was pushed aside.

At IBM, Lou Gerstner quickly did away with the highly orchestrated business planning meetings where executives came well prepared with data to present and defend their past performance. Instead, Gerstner required executives to prepare themselves by going out to the field for a few days and meeting in person with key client accounts, preferably those who had switched over to competitors.

Instead of following the established protocol of having each executive present their business unit results one at a time, he focused on critical issues that needed changing. By the end of the meeting, they had decided on changes, many of which were to be broadcast to all employees and the news media simultaneously, rather than communicated through IBM's multilayered chain of command. There was no room to hide or stall progress.

In stark contrast, strategic business meetings at the biggest change failures maintained a stale and polite tone. Disagreement was unwelcomed and was often seen as a sign of lack of loyalty. People listened to what others said and kept their opinions private. Warning signs and contradicting data were tolerated—barely—but never acted upon. Saving face and keeping in good standing was valued over getting results.

Getting a culturally diverse and politically divided group of executives to interact as a team can be difficult. Progress reviews at Crown Packaging started off on a bad note. The newly formed group of Crown executives, prior to being acquired by an integrated enterprise, ran their own companies. As such, some were former competitors. After the consolidation, trust remained low among this group of leaders and they were far from acting as an executive team.

Tom James brought the group together regularly to track business goals. He wanted to create the synergy of an integrated corporation. In preparation for these meetings, Tom asked each division to collect stakeholder feedback. Introducing stakeholder feedback as part of the strategic planning process was a radical notion.

Late one evening, after a dinner social and anticipating the strategic retreat the next morning, Tom, members of the SI team, and I contemplated how to help the executive team become more cohesive. While brainstorming options, we decided to take a risk and stir things. Next morning, each executive, joined by their respective leadership staff, was to stand in front of the other 12 division leaders and present not their division's results, but those of an assigned peer division instead.

The Crown executives were suspecting a more in-depth review as they had collected feedback from customers, employees, and suppliers in addition to the customary financial information. What they had not anticipated was that they were to analyze and make recommendations about another division. They knew nothing about their peers. How would they make comments on another division?

They had the entire morning and facilitators to prepare a sound business review based on the information provided. Needless to say, their curiosity to scrutinize their peer division's facts and figures was highly enticing. Ripping the other division apart in public would be tempting, but, of course, they were equally exposed. Taking a more collaborative approach, they dug into the data.

After intense preparations, division leaders checked assumptions and validated conclusions with the divisions they were about to represent. In a vigorous competitive spirit, each division did their best at presenting the good and the bad of their peer division. There was no room to hide. Transparency increased and decisions were tested. By the end of the retreat, former rivals had broken down communication barriers and were building relationships. As they began to exchange insights and best practices, the divisions began to truly collaborate.

The interactive approach to progress reviews continued for three consecutive years. In the process, Crown Packaging developed predictive models that linked stakeholder feedback to financial performance. The group became savvy at reading leading indicators from employee, customer, and supplier feedback. They asked to receive their assigned division's reports a week in advance of the progress reviews, so they could be better prepared and add value to their peer division.

The peer review helped division leaders learn from each other through stakeholder feedback. In addition, progress reviews included group discussions of leadership principles and best practices. Once they realized they had common goals, they learned to work as a team, creating the thinking, dialogue, and synergy necessary to improve profitability.

During progress reviews, leaders have a unique opportunity to air out issues, share ideas, review progress, and make important decisions. An effective forum encourages learning and exploration. An effective progress review ends with concrete decisions, specific assignments, and next steps.

To ensure that each progress review moves the team forward, it is critical to track results rather than activities. Results-oriented reports are tied to goals, people, and deadlines. The following chart contrasts the reporting format of results-oriented versus activity-oriented progress reviews.

RESULTS Reporting	ACTIVITY Reporting
Tied to measurable goals	Tied to activities
Tracks progress	Describes effort
Holds people accountable	Leaves out names
Brief and to the point	Elaborate and lengthy
Allows for trend analysis	Provides a historical review

Before adjourning, effective progress reviews define follow up actions to be achieved by the next milestone. Each participant leaves progress reviews with measurable goals, clear assignments, and specific results pertaining to their organization. The information needs to be readily available to all managers so they can see how their performance compares with other groups and how it aligns with the overall company objectives. Transparency accelerates informed decisions and increases accountability.

Following progress reviews, the team leader could send a message to the participants that summarizes the key points of agreement and confirms their commitment. The leader may ask each person to reply with their agreement. This follow up may invite additional feedback that may not have been expressed during the meeting. Those bringing up additional feedback still need to indicate their commitment and, if willing, present it before the entire group at the next meeting. This process allows the leader to confirm full support and hold others accountable for results.

The way to get started is
to quit talking and begin doing.

~Walt Disney

Making Transformations Incrementally

Continuous improvement is about making steady progress. Organizations make big changes by a series of incremental innovations. The 10 most successful organizational changes show that a series of minor adjustments and incremental innovations added up over time to a big transformational change. A close examination of how change actually happens reveals the enduring power of evolution.

In 1909 Benjamin Holt bought an abandoned tractor manufacturing plant. For several years he had been experimenting with farming uses of steam-powered tractors. The problem he encountered, however, was that the heavy machines often got bogged down in the soft soil. Once stuck, they proved very difficult to pull free, even with teams of horses.

A common solution at that time was to lay a temporary plank road ahead of the steam tractor. Holt came up with a better idea: carry the road with the vehicle. To prove his concept, he placed wooden, block-linked treads around the idlers on Holt No. 77, his test tractor. The results were impressive, and the modern tractor was born. By 1911, Holt's factory employed 625 workers and sold tractors in the United States, Argentina, Mexico, and Canada.

It wasn't until 1925 that Caterpillar was officially formed. The newly formed company was initially hit hard by the economic crash of 1929. During the post-war years, however, Caterpillar boomed as a result of ambitious reconstruction campaigns to help rebuild Europe and Japan. Since then, the company has managed to systematically expand its operations through the ups and downs of the world economy. Currently, Caterpillar operates a large network of manufacturing factories, suppliers, and dealers in multiple industries and across over 200 countries.

The year 2007 marked a milestone. It represented the fourth consecutive year of double-digit growth with record sales and profit for Caterpillar. Favorable economic conditions fostered that growth. Even so, what makes this recent success particularly impressive is that it required a big company to make multiple large-scale changes simultaneously.

In the period between 2003 to 2007 Caterpillar made seven major acquisitions, reduced operational costs, improved quality, and introduced the Caterpillar Production System, a mechanism for integrating operations, culture, and management. There was also a change in leadership, as James W. Owens succeeded Glen A. Barton.

Assimilating so many changes influenced Caterpillar's culture significantly. "Simply put, Caterpillar is not the same company we were 10 years ago," commented former CEO Barton.

In only four years, Caterpillar netted a 264% appreciation in stock price, an increase of $38,583 million in company value, and over 32,000 additional jobs. We cannot attribute such gains solely to favorable economic conditions, since Caterpillar outpaced the S&P 500 index for its industry. Plotting the financial

Caterpillar

Stock Price between 2003 and 2007

Close price adjusted for dividends and splits

impact of all the changes Caterpillar went through between 2003 and 2007 shows a steady climb with minor bumps along the way—the Path of Ascent!

Caterpillar is clearly one the 10 most successful changes of the last 15 years. Looking at the outcome, one may expect to see the introduction of a bold new vision, a clever strategic direction, a distinctive leadership style, or big growth initiative. There is no grand strategic change. No landmark event. Not even a sense of innovative shift. During that eventful four-year period at Caterpillar, there was no silver bullet that can explain their achievements.

Caterpillar did try a lot of things, but the changes were part of an ongoing, long-term improvement process. Even the CEO succession followed the long tradition of promoting and developing leaders from within company ranks. CEO and Chairman James W. Owens joined Caterpillar as a corporate economist right out of college. For over 35 years, he advanced through a variety of global management positions. When he was appointed to the lead position in February 2004, Owens continued to build on his predecessor's direction and initiatives.

What one can easily notice by reading press releases, journal articles, financial figures, and company announcements between 2003 and 2007 is a relentless focus on growth. Focused, disciplined, and steady effort was what made Caterpillar transform successfully in a relatively short period of time. From an internal perspective, these changes were so incremental that most employees would say they were simply doing their jobs. As one employee put it, "We were just building great machines. That's all!"

The Change Masters achieved vast changes and introduced radical innovations incrementally—steadily improving, keeping what worked and discarding what didn't. Their success is more the result of trial and error than the result of one "Big Bang" idea. The difference between those that ultimately succeed and those that didn't is their ability to build up improvements over time to eventually amount to big gains.

> *Nature does constant value stream mapping—*
> *it's called evolution.*
>
> ~Carrie Latet

Achieving Personal Excellence

So far, the focus has been on how organizations achieve increasingly better results. The principles of setting goals, identifying performance indicators, and continuous improvement apply to individuals as well. It takes deliberate practice to get better at anything.

In virtually every field, most people learn quickly at first, but then slow down and after a while, usually completely stop developing. We often find people in jobs with 20 years of first-year experience. Little was gained beyond the initial learning curve. Some, however, continue to improve for years and even decades and go on to greatness. The most reliable predictor of success is persistent and steady practice over time. The profile of top performers in sports, finance, and performing arts illustrates how purposeful practice works.

Tiger Woods was introduced to golf by his father at the extremely early age of 18 months. He was encouraged to practice intensively, building an advantage of no less than 15 years of practice by the time he became the youngest winner of the U.S. Amateur Championship. Woods continued his tireless pursuit of excellence in golfing well into his adult career, devoting many hours a day to conditioning and practice. Never satisfied with his already great performance, he twice took six months off his busy career to remake his swing. Before each upgrade break, Tiger was already known for a powerful swing. Tiger went on improving an area where he was already one of the best because that was what it would take for him to get even better.

Warren Buffett, known for his wizardry in picking stocks, may come across as someone gifted with the Midas touch. Reviewing his life tells a different story. As the son of a local stockbroker, Buffett was exposed to stock markets at a very young age. Buffett began studying financial statements an early age, meticulously analyzing the potential impact of different investments from his father's business. He advanced his investing philosophy from Benjamin Graham, an early career mentor and one of the leading investors of his time. Buffet credits Graham with grounding him in the investment framework that made him successful. Buffett openly admits that he invests only in companies he fully understands, often devoting long hours to analyzing trends and learning all he can about a company and its industry. At age 78, he continues to judiciously practice the investment discipline that made him one of the greatest investors.

In football, all-time-great receiver Jerry Rice, who was passed up by 15 teams because they considered him too slow, practiced so hard that other players would get sick trying to keep up with him. Vladimir Horowitz supposedly said, "If I don't practice for a day, I know it. If I don't practice for two days, my wife knows it. If I don't practice for three days, the world knows it."

Practice makes perfect. Researchers are finding that it takes approximately 10,000 hours of practice to achieve the level of mastery we often link with elite performers. It turns out that even those deemed to be genius have accrued their proficiency over roughly 10,000 hours of diligent performance. It takes an enormous amount of practice to become excellent.

Of course, not every person that practices a discipline for 10 years becomes excellent at it. It is not the rote repetition of doing the same thing over and over that builds capacity. Dr. K. Anders Ericsson, who studies expert performers, points out that "just because you've been walking for 55 years doesn't mean you're getting better at it." Achieving proficiency is about deliberate practice, having the discipline to reach increasingly higher goals.

Practice without improvement is meaningless.

~Chuck Knox

To understand how business professionals can engage in deliberate practice, we can take the example of medical diagnosticians. Typically, medical diagnosticians see a patient once or twice, make an assessment in an effort to solve a particular problem, and then move on. They may never see that patient again or revisit the case. Getting used to such a routine tends to limit the diagnosticians' learning. Over time, they develop a habit for giving similar prescriptions to similar cases, and assuming a satisfactory accuracy.

In an interview with a highly successful diagnostician, Dr. Ericsson describes how the top performers work very differently. At the time of initial diagnosis, these diagnosticians took extensive notes on the patient's condition. At the following patient visit, they spent additional time checking up on their patient's response. Before the day's end, they went back through their patient's records to check the accuracy of their initial diagnoses, noting any discrepancies, errors, and successes.

Over time, the top diagnosticians increased their accuracy by noticing small variations and subtle hints in the different situations. More importantly, they were still learning, never quite satisfied with their skill level. They created for themselves a feedback loop that gave them a performance edge.

For managers whose daily activities cover a full spectrum of human interactions, achieving excellence may seem overwhelming. How can one master the multiple disciplines of management? It may seem like what John McEnroe said on losing to Tim Mayotte in a professional indoor tennis championship:

"This taught me a lesson, but I'm not sure what it is." In order to grow, managers need to identify and measure specific skills.

When broken down into specific competencies, a manager's job can be mastered through incremental improvement. The difference between top performers and average leaders at one of my clients was measured to be only about 10%. As we observed the very best managers in their daily interactions, we noticed how they delegated an assignment, responded to a sharp remark, or asked for feedback before making a decision. Collectively, these seemingly small details amounted to what others recognized as excellent leadership.

Not everyone is necessarily interested in becoming a top performer. However, most people are interested in getting better at something. Whatever it is that we want to do better, it takes deliberate practice to improve. Inside every good person there is an even better one trying to come out. Improving results is the aim that makes all the effort worthwhile.

That which we persist in doing becomes easier
as we do it; not that the nature of the thing changes,
but the power to do becomes greater.

~ Ralph Waldo Emerson

Chapter Review

Summary

A successful change is focused on results, not activities. This can be done by identifying and tracking the key performance indicators with the greatest impact on the outcome. Tracking progress toward specific milestones helps create early wins, boosting confidence and support. Continuous progress comes from measuring and reporting performance indicators regularly. Progress reviews provide the forum for evaluating results and making course corrections as needed. The discipline of regular reporting performance measures builds accountability where results continuously improve.

Key Points

- Continuous improvements account for significant gains over time.
- The greatest gains come from identifying, measuring, and analyzing key indicators.
- Achieving early wins within 100 days or less builds confidence in the success of a change initiative.
- Accountability is established by confirming a mutual agreement to specific commitments and then regularly tracking progress.
- Effective progress reviews report on results that tie goals to people and deadlines.
- Deliberate practice is required for achieving excellence in any field of endeavor.

Group Discussion

1. What specific results does our team want to achieve in the next 100 days?
2. What are the key performance indicators?
3. How effective are we at tracking progress?
4. How can we increase accountability for results?

Access additional Ascent Tools at
www.ascent-advisor.com/tools.html

## PART THREE

Turning Vision into Reality

## CHAPTER NINE

Making the Ascent

The miracle is not that we do this work,
but that we are so happy doing it.

~ Mother Theresa

Checking Your Backpack

In a world of growing distrust, uncertainty, and tensions, it is nothing short of a miracle for an individual, a team, or an organization to make the Ascent. Yet the principles described in the previous five chapters are applied every day by ordinary people who are making real progress in their lives and at work. The focus of this chapter is to describe how this simple process actually works.

Before we start on the Ascent, let's check what is in our backpack. In other words, what unnecessary baggage are we bringing on? We may need to repack our bags with the proper gear. We may be carrying heavy weights that will burden us, drag us down, and eventually disqualify us altogether from making a successful climb. Let's start by checking our motives.

What makes the Ascent different than traditional approaches to change is the underlying motive. The object of the Ascent is not getting something we want, but doing something for the well-being of others, including ourselves. Acting this way may not come naturally to any of us, and especially for the organizations where we work. We can't justify this. We need to elevate our motives before we can lift ourselves and the organization.

We need not rush to claim altruistic feelings that we do not yet have. That would be hypocritical and doomed to fail because others will eventually detect our real intentions. All we need to do is to elevate our aim. As we act for the greater good, placing other's interests ahead of our own, we cultivate nobler aspirations.

On the Ascent, a leader can give directions and make requests from others, but cannot make demands or impose his will on others. That would stop the flow of commitment required to grow. The Ascent respects the other people's freedom.

Leading with firmness and conviction does not mean imposing one's will by force. The Ascent does not force others to give more of their time, attention, or energy, but persuades others through personal mastery, knowledge, and sincere respect.

Perhaps the greatest leadership comes when we resist the impulse to become upset or offended when someone has let us down. When we don't judge or criticize another person for their shortcomings, but correct with patience and accuracy, we are most influential and powerful. Effective leadership is based on respect, understanding, acceptance, appreciation, and trust.

Respect is to value another person's freedom to choose. Respecting another person requires recognizing someone else's choices, strengths, and virtues even when they are different from our own.

Understanding is to want to know the other person better, taking additional time to listen, observe, and communicate at a personal level. Understanding requires time and energy invested in getting to know others. This investment pays great dividends as we are able to rely on others more fully.

Acceptance is to free ourselves from making demands and placing expectations on others. It does not mean that we compromise our goals or values, but that we respect someone else's. It does not mean that we become permissive, but that we allow others the right to act. It does not mean that one has to be wrong for the other to be right. You can be who you are and allow others the same right.

Appreciation is to value differences of opinion as an essential enrichment in the relationship. Accepting others requires faith and courage, especially when their choices affect us adversely. By accepting others, we gain their voluntary commitment when we do work together.

Trust is relying on each other. Giving of ourselves and receiving other's contributions helps create an interdependent relationship of trust. To trust is to act with confidence that things will turn out without any need to fear or control the outcome. Fear and trust cannot coexist, because the presence of one dispels the other. The more we trust, the less we fear.

Trusting others and trusting ourselves are not alternatives, but two sides of the same coin. The way we treat others says more about ourselves than about the others. On the Ascent, people can achieve better results simply because they treat each other the way they want to be treated. The Golden Rule is the standard for high performance.

As we ponder about what it takes to make the Ascent, take some time to check what is in your bag. Disposing of faulty assumptions and harmful motives will free you from unnecessary burdens. Moreover, it will allow you to lift off. Then you are ready to start making your Personal Ascent.

Starting the Personal Ascent

Improving an organization starts by improving ourselves. The principles and practices we wish to share with others need to be demonstrated in our conduct. For Wayne, improving the paper manufacturing operation under his control required him to take on a Personal Ascent.

There were three things Wayne was absolutely sure about. One: He had a great job. Two: He was doing a really good job. Three: If he didn't change, he would lose everything!

The thought of losing everything he had worked so hard to build over most of his lifetime was almost too much to bear. It meant a major setback for his career, a shock to his peers, and the resulting embarrassment at work. He would have to deal with a much larger loss, both financially and in his personal life. He was about to lose his wife of 15 years as well. Leaving with her would be irreplaceable memories and family moments. All this and more he would face because of an insidious personality flaw that affected most people he knew. He was an authoritarian, controlling, micromanaging type of boss.

Being overcontrolling had been a mixed blessing for Wayne. At least, that is how he thought of his demanding expectations. On one hand, he had been steadily promoted at work with increasing responsibilities because he was hard driving and willing to take charge. On the other hand, his actions chased away people, often really good ones, who would no longer take his obsessive compulsion for control. He preferred to use the word *perfectionist* to describe his tendency, since it conveyed a touch of virtue.

However you look at it, Wayne was at a crossroads at work and in his life. He found himself involved in the middle of a cultural transformation at Crown Packaging, bombarded with leadership training, 360-degree feedback, and coaching. He could no longer plunge ahead, as he usually had, ignoring the feedback. He had to change.

In order to change, Wayne realized he needed some help. A group of change champions and I were brought in to help Wayne and his organization turn around. The operation was losing money, chronically unable to meet quality and on-time delivery standards. After a comprehensive assessment, we concluded that Wayne himself was a root cause for many of the problems.

His approach to running the operation was not allowing people the latitude to make decisions. And while Wayne had usually been making most of the decisions in the past, he was no longer able to keep up with the pace of change. Further complicating the situation, personal life challenges where mounting, causing increased anxiety and stress. Something had to give!

"What do you really want?" I asked Wayne pointedly.

"I want to continue to lead operations successfully like I have in the past. All these changes are making my work quite impossible," Wayne replied, rather contentiously.

"Can we go back to the way things were before?" I questioned.

Wayne shook his head while staring at the floor. "It seems that we can't," he confessed.

"How else can you lead a successful operation?" I continued.

"I guess we can try this empowerment thing," he said reluctantly. "There will be mistakes," he warned me, "costly mistakes, because this is a complex operation and the people are not well trained." Then, Wayne brought up deeper issues. "I have to earn the trust of the workers on the floor," he admitted. "Several of them don't really like me and won't support this change." Wayne was starting to open up.

"How could you increase trust with your employees? What exactly would you need to do differently?" I probed further into Wayne's personal change.

Over the following two hours Wayne and I outlined a plan for increasing trust at the plant. His enthusiasm grew as he saw how he would be able to lead the process. It started with Wayne and his team defining a common purpose, creating a shared vision of success. Then they set goals and crafted a plan for achieving them. They asked for feedback from customers and employees. Wayne personally provided abundant training and coaching aimed at increasing the workforce knowledge. He delegated responsibilities for measuring and improving performance to the team leaders.

Within a few months production was up. In the process, costly mistakes occurred with the consequent loss of key client accounts. But total sales grew, as the operation was becoming more competitive. In the course of the changes, Wayne had become a new person.

Seeing Wayne go through this process was an amazing experience. He abandoned painful practices in favor of more effective ones. Even his appearance changed, as he quit his long-standing addiction to smoking and got in better physical shape. Learning to empower others not only improved Wayne's organization, but gave new life to his struggling marriage. Wayne's personal change resulted in a sustainable change for himself, his work, and his life.

Many leaders have learned to manage from role models who are not good examples of leadership. Their poor habits have been reinforced by immediate results, and they have not realized that far better results were possible.

The Five Ascent Principles provide the foundation for leading personal and organizational change. Put it to the test! Think of something you really want to achieve at work or in your personal life. It can be an inspiring dream of success or abandoning a bad habit that holds you back. Be specific about the change you want to see happen.

Put your book down, and think about what you want to improve most in your life. Take your time. Don't rush through. Write down specifically what you want to improve. Then review the Ascent process, step by step. The framework below can guide you through the steps.

The Five Questions
For Improving Personal Performance

ENVISION: What do I what to see happen?
- Describe desired outcomes
- Define my guiding principles
- How others' needs align with my own

Outcome: Build Common Purpose

EVALUATE: How can I make it happen?
- Define what is happening now
- Set meaningful goals
- Outline an action plan

Outcome: Clarify Direction

EMPOWER: How do I build on strengths?
- Develop personal strengths
- Overcome potential derailers
- Define a process for improvement

Outcome: Develop Capacity

ENGAGE: How do I inspire myself to act?
- Identify what motivates me
- Create the conditions to stay committed
- Ask for coaching and feedback

Outcome: Inspire Commitment

EVOLVE: How do I track progress?
- Deliver on early wins
- Track performance indicators
- Review progress towards 100-day goals

Outcome: Achieve Results

Access additional Ascent Tools at
www.ascent-advisor.com/tools.html

You may need some quiet, uninterrupted time to answer these questions thoroughly. Make sure you do take the time, now or soon. The outcome can be life-changing!

Start by creating your personal story of success. What kind of person do you want to be? This is profound and the most important aspect of harnessing a powerful purpose for change. Write down your personal mission. Then describe how you will fulfill that mission. Write down your personal vision and describe how you will get there. The process of clarifying one's purpose takes time and energy, but helps us develop the faith and courage to overcome seemingly impossible challenges and achieve powerful goals.

Achieving such goals will require changing. This is the time to get realistic and decide how you are going to achieve your goals. Trace an action plan describing exactly what you are going to do differently: What you will stop doing and what you will start doing instead. Before completing this step, ask others for feedback on your action plan.

With clear purpose and direction, it is time to build ability and motivation to make the plan real. Identify strengths you need to develop, allocating time and resources for acquiring specialized skills. You may also want to include other people who need to play a role in helping you achieve the goal.

Keeping yourself engaged through the ups and downs of a change process is important. You will need to create the conditions to stay motivated over time. Anticipate setbacks and plan in advance how to respond and recover. Surround yourself with positive influences. The association with others who are progressing will help you keep on track.

While going after a personal transformation, you will need to invest in the immediate early wins. Set milestones for the first 100 days of the change, keeping track of your progress. Celebrate each victory and quickly recover from setbacks. As you do these things, you will see immediate and consistent progress toward your desired goal.

Fortunately for Wayne, he was able to make a noticeable change that helped him regain the confidence of colleagues at work and family members. This personal change qualified Wayne to later become instrumental to leading a turnaround at his organization that benefitted hundreds of employees. Overcoming ineffective behaviors often leads to greater opportunities at work and in other areas of life.

Changing deeply entrenched habits often requires outside help from someone who knows how to assist you, or who knows how to overcome challenges similar to the ones you are facing. Personal change is the source of organizational change. Taking a team to a higher level follows a similar process.

Leading the Team Upwards

Recently, one of my clients told me about a troubled customer service team at her financial services firm. For years, several managers had tried to improve customer service, but despite their many efforts, the team continued to experience poor results, recurring errors, and complaints. After going through three different managers in two years, the team was demoralized and had become a dead-end at the company.

"What have these managers tried to do?" I asked curiously.

"They've tried everything!" she said, hopelessly. "They upgraded the computer system, they trained everyone, they fired some of the poor performers, and they introduced incentives. So far, nothing has worked."

I was surprised at the list of failed initiatives that had been tried with no apparent gain. "What do the customer service employees say is the problem?"

"They blame management, of course," she said without giving any credence to their claim.

"I assume that you and the rest of the company believe that the customer service employees are the problem."

"Obviously," she stated, agitatedly. "Who else?"

"So everything has been tried so far to change them and all you get is resistance," I concluded.

"Exactly!" she exclaimed.

"Let me take a shot at customer service. I think I might know what will work with them," I proposed confidently. "I bet that by now they know full well how to fix themselves."

She was skeptical, but gave me the opportunity, realizing that there was little harm in trying again.

I asked for a single day offsite for a planning meeting with just the team members. The manager and the company president were invited to kick off the meeting and then come back at the end of the day to hear the action plan. I asked the leaders to fully support the team's decisions.

In a single day, the team went from resistance to active participation. Follow-up with this group 30 days after the workshop indicated they were still making strong progress. Sixty days after the workshop, they were still getting better. Ninety days later, many people at the company were talking about the noticable change in customer services. A full six months later, people inside and outside the team agreed that something had happened that made a big difference.

The magnitude of what was achieved that one day surprised me as well. Looking back at that eventful day, I can clearly see the Ascent Process at work. Since everyone had given up on this team, I decided to drop all my expectations. I was willing to help them as their facilitator in whatever they wanted to do. As they realized they were in charge of making the changes, they took off.

Let's review this team's Ascent Process step by step. In this case, rather than start with rehashing the department's many problems, we started brainstorming the vision for the department. They all wanted to do their best to serve the customer. Great! What does that mean? They described the ideal interaction with customers and other departments. They were cynical at first, but as they realized the possibilities, they became excited about doing things better for everyone.

After envisioning for a few hours, we moved into evaluating the current situation, paying special attention to seizing the opportunities for change. Every obstacle was to be reframed as an opportunity, instead of a barrier to making progress. A list of

10 to 12 items was condensed into three core strategic objectives. The focus was frequently redirected to the desired goal rather than the problems.

In the afternoon, we moved into empowering key players based on their strengths. Trust in managers was a sore point, as they had experienced much friction with their leaders and other departments in the company. Rather than dwell on blaming the absent, they had to make a case for how they wanted to be led. It became clear that one of the customer service representatives had been doing all the work of managing the department without any of the recognition or authority. Formalizing this role, I thought, would be doable if the aspiring leader was able to demonstrate leadership skills.

Later in the afternoon, we discussed engaging the team members. They did not care for incentives that were outside of their control or for motivational hype. Both of these approaches had been attempted unsuccessfully before. What they wanted was peer collaboration and respect from other departments. Projecting the proper attitude toward the rest of the company would eventually give them just that.

Before the end of the day, we decided how to evolve this process, translating goals into specific performance measures and assignments. Team members were excited about the day's outcome. So was I. Much had been accomplished in a single day. Before concluding, they presented their plan to their manager and the company president. It was well received. Such public commitment held them accountable to deliver on the plan. To everyone's surprise, customer services made good on their improvement actions without delay.

The framework on the next page describes the types of questions a team would go through facilitating the Ascent Process in a single meeting. The buy-in of individual team members is essential to a successful outcome. The change process can be facilitated by the manager, but it cannot be imposed.

Facilitating the Ascent Process for a large organization requires additional time and resources. For example, more than a single day will be necessary to address the purpose, direction,

The Five Questions
For Improving Team Performance

ENVISION: What do we what to see happen?
- Describe desired outcomes
- Define guiding principles
- Align stakeholders needs

Outcome: Build Common Purpose

EVALUATE: How can we make it happen?
- Analyze the current situation
- Set strategic goals
- Create an action plan

Outcome: Clarify Direction

EMPOWER: How do we build on strengths?
- Deploy change champions
- Develop core competencies
- Define a process to work more effectively

Outcome: Develop Capacity

ENGAGE: How do we inspire collaboration?
- Create the conditions for engagement
- Facilitate teamwork
- Coach for high performance

Outcome: Inspire Commitment

EVOLVE: How do we track progress?
- Deliver on early wins
- Track key performance indicators
- Review progress towards 100-day goals

Outcome: Achieve Results

Access additional Ascent Tools at
www.ascent-advisor.com/tools.html

ability, motivation, and results of an organization made up of departments and functions. Input from various sources, inside and outside the organization, will be necessary to gain an objective perspective and make sound decisions. Yet the overall process remains the same.

Implementation is the key for turning vision into results. The actual Ascent Plan is ultimately less valuable than the planning process itself. The discipline of implementing the steps while practicing the principles is what creates the desired results. The Ascent Plan becomes a guiding framework for ongoing improvement.

*Planning is bringing the future into the present
so that you can do something about it now.*

~Alan Lakein

Scoping the Next 100 Days

Where do we start making progress? The starting point is creating the Ascent Plan, outlining the organizational change process. The Ascent Plan evaluates an organization's purpose, direction, ability, motivation, and results. The 5Es Model provides the framework for initiating the Ascent.

Getting started requires effective timing of events. A slow start kills motivation and leads to slow implementation. Before long, the initial excitement vanishes and people lose commitment as the initiative representing change becomes part of the status quo.

A 100-day plan communicates the urgency necessary to make things happen. A decisive pace creates momentum and commitment that accelerate the pace of change. It is also important to keep the project manageable. Budgets and resources are more readily available and approvals become simpler to obtain if the scope of change is contained within 100 days. Before everyone starts questioning a change, the initial results are on their way.

The scope needs to target results big enough to matter and small enough to be achievable. As a general rule, it is better to be successful on a smaller scale and expand later than to tackle too much too soon and have to retrench later. Leaders can gain buy-in for larger changes by launching smaller projects that deliver encouraging results within 100 days or less.

The 100-day scope does not compromise larger scale objectives. The 5Es Model can be used to define the full scope of a long-term change project up front. Then the master project can be broken down into subprojects that deliver initial gains toward the larger objectives. Each subproject moves through the five

The Ascent Process
5Es for Mastering Change

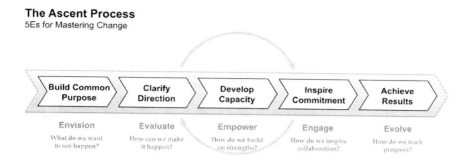

steps to achieve results with 100 days or less. The initial results can be evaluated and adjustments made before launching additional projects. Rather than hoping for a big payout in some distant future, the 100-day, results-oriented approach to long-term change ensures successes along the way.

In order to make timely progress, each 100-day project moves through the five steps. The steps build on each other, as they provide the foundation for the next step. A change process that is out of sequence creates disjointed activities. People may end up doing the wrong things, or doing the right things for the wrong reasons. For example, they may be inspired to work as a team, only to learn later on that the team is being restructured.

The 5Es Model describes the proper sequence. For each step there is a corresponding principle. Each principle is implemented through specific practices that result in a predictable outcome.

Make no little plans; they have no magic to stir men's blood.
Make big plans, aim high and work hard.

~Daniel H. Burnham

Implementing the Ascent Plan

To illustrate how the Ascent Plan works in real life, we will use the case of a hospital emergency room. Daily crises are the norm, and work is often a matter of life or death. Patients wait to be treated—some with serious conditions; others with minor trauma. The area is overcrowded, especially during peak hours.

Nurses buzz around busily triaging patients, sometimes even in the hallways. Doctors pace from patient to patient checking their vital signs, while making small talk and deciding the best diagnosis. Overall, things are a bit hectic at the ER.

Invisible to the patients, however, is the frustration the staff feels as they face budget cuts that result in lower staffing levels, cause longer patient waiting times, and add stress. Nurses say they were in a scramble before the economy hit, and now they are in a mad scramble. A resident physician in the ER agrees, saying that there is no time to communicate with other departments. They feel locked down in survival mode, just doing their jobs, not realizing how they are affecting everybody else. The sad consequence is that some patients linger in pain longer while others may be misdiagnosed.

One nurse, Joanne, interned at the emergency room while she was an undergraduate nursing student. She decided then to make emergency medicine her career. After graduation, Joanne took a staff nursing position at the same hospital's ER.

Soon, Joanne began taking additional responsibilities as the staff began turning to her for help thinning overcrowded situations. Her sharp organization and decision-making skills proved indispensable in making sure they had beds for incoming patients. "I felt it was my duty to do something to help the situation," Joanne said. But the budget cuts made her job almost impossible, as the hospital was experiencing increasing shortages.

The ER director position had been vacant for several months, and previous directors had lasted less than a year. With no one in charge, the ER was in constant chaos. "Why don't you apply for the position?" one of her colleagues questioned. "We need a leader and you understand us." Joanne decided to take a few days off to think things through.

The 5Es Model provided Joanne a framework to decide what she really wanted and how to obtain it. "What is the story of success?" Joanne wondered. She wrote down her ideal career path, including envisioned events in her personal and family life. "How can I seize the opportunity?" was her second question. Joanne drew up a plan with specific goals and a timeline. Following the model, she decided to ask her husband and colleagues for feedback before committing to the specifics.

Then Joanne proceeded to identify how to develop her strengths as a leader and in her staff. Her guiding criteria was to identify what talent was needed where, and who was really good at doing what. She decided she wanted to receive the additional leadership training offered by the hospital. Building teamwork and commitment with her staff was going to be the biggest challenge. Being relatively new to the department, Joanne recognized, would not bode well with the older staff.

Joanne outlined an action plan with set milestones and a follow-up process to keep her on track. She knew that back on the job, many competing priorities would vie for her attention. She wanted to stay focused and see improvement. Instinctively, she knew that nothing would speak louder than results.

Joanne was formally offered the position as interim director of the ER. She accepted and began to address the department's chronic troubles. Following the same five-step process, Joanne initiated staff meetings every two weeks to address root problems. The focus was on delivering quality care to an increasing patient volume with fewer staff. At first, all the staff could do was vent and complain about what seemed a hopeless situation. After listening to a few gripe sessions, Joanne asked them to stop focusing on the problem and envision the ideal situation. That startled the group.

With my assistance as a facilitator and the participation of physicians and other department representatives, the group came up with an idealistic yet attainable vision. Surprisingly, their vision had little to do with improving work processes or additional staffing. Instead, the vision focused on improving relationships between workers. They envisioned an environment where everyone would treat each other with civility and respect. In the envisioned ER, new nurses would thrive and learn from the older ones. The more established nurses would share their knowledge and encourage others' advancement. Apparently, this type of interaction was not present and was blocking further progress.

The group was asked to turn the envisioned ER into a story they could tell to each other. The story became catchy and rumors spread through the hospital about the "ER of the future." The staff began taking ownership of the story and adopting new behaviors as if they were already heading in that direction.

Following the 5Es Model, Joanne moved the team through a plan of action with objectives to make the vision real. They identified key players inside and outside the organization with the skills and influence to make change happen. They shifted some people around and sent the most respected nurses to leadership training.

The landmark event occurred during the course of a workshop addressing the drivers of engagement. Presented with peer feedback, the group finally broached the undiscussable subject of cliques. Over the years, the older nurses had formed a strong clique. Inadvertently or intentionally, the informal power of this group left the younger nurses feeling disempowered. The silent group finally spoke up. Fully aware of the situation, Joanne decided to set higher standards for the ER to work as one team.

Working more unitedly and with a solid game plan, they were able to reorganize the flow of traffic in the emergency area and create additional areas for triage. Doctors noticed the change in the staff and began acting more respectfully toward the nurses. Together they came up with a triage process that almost doubled the number of patients they could treat during peak hours. The ER changes caught the attention of the hospital administration.

The chief nursing officer asked Joanne to present to the hospital leaders how they achieved the noticeable improvements. The overcrowded, understaffed situation at the ER was far from solved, Joanne pointed out, but there was a positive, in-charge feeling among the staff. She described the 5Es Model and then proposed to the administration how they could help the ER. Joanne asked the senior leaders to address broader ER needs. She proposed going through the 5Es Model to get an action plan in place.

The scope now involved leaders inside and outside the hospital. The issues were much more complex, but the Ascent Process remained simple and effective. The vision was for the hospital to reach out to growing communities with dispersed clinics. The plan required funding, feasibility studies, and competitive analysis. Hospital leaders launched a public relations and media campaign to educate the local community on the healthcare services provided at various locations in the community. Incoming patients were triaged upon arrival and directed to the most suitable care area. The hospital expanded emergency services through scaled-down basic care walk-in clinics. The ER workload was no longer a hopeless case.

Joanne would simply say that they have made a lot of progress, but there is still room for improvement. Not one single change or momentous decision suddenly made everything better, but the overall condition of the ER was vastly improved. The change process facilitated a common vision, based on values and focused on results for improving emergency medicine.

The premise of this book is that change yields a predictable positive outcome when it is based on the Five Ascent Principles. The choice is made from the start. The process reinforces the initial conditions, making the eventual success foreseeable from the beginning. The key is to take the right path for the right reasons.

Plans are only good intentions unless they immediately degenerate into hard work.

~Peter Drucker

## CHAPTER TEN

Ascending in the Worst of Times

Prosperity is a great teacher; adversity a greater.

~William Hazlitt

Rising from the Fall

Up to this point, the stories describing the Path of Ascent have been based on examples of the recent past. Some may point out that the favorable conditions of the last few decades enabled most companies to expand with little restraint. Those conditions have changed. Facing the worst economy in modern history leaves people wondering if growth is still possible. These days, most companies are struggling just to survive, posing the poignant question if it is feasible to ascend during a downturn.

Now, more than ever, there is an imperative need to ascend if we are to rise again. Examples from the past provide valuable lessons for us today. In October 1929 the crash of financial markets ushered in a decade of despair and depression for the United States and the world. How the most successful leaders and companies responded then provides a useful framework for us today.

Throughout the Roaring Twenties, businesses had overextended themselves due to irresponsible lending and excessive spending. The era was characterized by rampant consumerism, technological breakthroughs, and declining social values. On Wall Street, investors came to believe that markets had reached the point where they could sustain high levels indefinitely. In a few tumultuous days before the end of the decade, markets long fed by unrealistic expectations suddenly collapsed, like a house of cards. The financial crash of 1929 triggered a wave of business failures, starting with reputable financial institutions and spreading to all sectors of the economy.

Public attitudes changed as abruptly as the forces that dragged the economy downward. Business executives, once acclaimed for their bold risk taking, soon became disparaged as the primary culprits of frivolous spending and irrational greed. What was considered innovative and courageous during the 1920s was quickly deemed unethical and foolhardy. Reputable firms whose names were held in high esteem suddenly became tarnished by scandal and accusations of predatory practices.

Almost all businesses did poorly during the first three years immediately following the market crash. The only companies that continued to grow while thousands of others faltered were those able to capitalize in the shifting trends. To little credit of their own, certain industries were simply recession-proof. During the hardest times people continued to consume food, use cosmetics, and spend on entertainment. Unable to indulge in more expensive luxuries, consumers turned to simpler, still affordable pleasures that gave them temporary relief from their pressing reality.

Beyond the few recession-resistant niches, all other industries saw major losses during the three years following the fall of 1929. Even the best companies' stocks fell as the market went south. Benjamin Graham, the renowned value investor of the time, lost 60% during those three years. The widespread loss of confidence in financial institutions caused an economic contraction that gripped the world for a decade. The stock market reveals the typical profile of the Roller Coaster Ride during the six years following the onset of the Great Depression.

The Roller Coaster Ride

The Stock Market at the Onset of the Great Depression

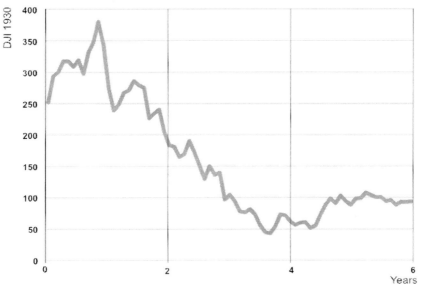

Dow Jones Industrial Average (DJI) from Oct. 1928 to Oct. 1934
Scale on the left from 0 to 400 points

Anyone who bought stocks in mid-1929
and held onto them saw most of his or her
adult life pass by before getting back to even.

~Richard M. Salsman

Not everyone remained on the Roller Coaster Ride for the entire span of the Depression. After markets hit bottom, some individuals and companies began to grow quickly, even if they were not in recession-proof industries. Not only did they recover, but these organizations prospered greatly. What the winning organizations did during the downturn determined, to a great extent, how well they came out after the Depression.

The Depression Beaters show the top performing company stocks in terms of total return from among the 150 prominent NYSE stocks. Individually, these companies represent a variety

Depression Beaters		
Company	Industry	Total Returns
1. Sloss Sheffield	Steel/Iron	1476.08%
2. American Crystal Sugar	Sugar	1155.46%
3. United States Rubber	Rubber	1143.48%
4. Cerro De Pasco Copper	Copper	844.32%
5. Sears Roebuck	Retail	753.30%
6. American Metal Ltd.	Metal Products	739.27%
7. Coca Cola	Beverages	704.76%
8. United States Pipe/Fdry.	Iron	702.12%
9. Bethlehem Steel	Steel	682.60%
10. General Motors	Auto Maker	680.21%

Depression Beaters represent the top performing stocks in terms of total return from
market bottom on Feb 28, 1933, to Feb 29, 1940, from among the 150 prominent NYSE
stocks listed in the January, 1, 1925, issue of *Forbes Magazine*.

Calculated based on data from CRSP US Stock Database © 2009 Center for Research in
Security Prices (CRSP). The University of Chicago Booth School of Business.

of industries and backgrounds; collectively they prove an important point. Their rise from the market bottom in 1933 was sustained for the seven years of the Depression until 1940 and
beyond. Essentially, for these companies, there was no Depression. Their example leaves no doubt as to our current ability to
get on the Path of Ascent during the current decline.

Through the bleak days of the Great Depression, the companies that eventually prospered increased efficiency in a way
that made them stronger. The most successful firms didn't
just cut costs. They became efficiency innovators by investing in technology, redefining worker relationships, engaging
entrepreneurial drive, restoring trust with stakeholders, and
strengthening core operations. Their counterparts, on the
other hand, were progressively weakened by recurring waves
of cost reduction.

> # Efficiency innovations made organizations stronger during the downturn.

Investing in Technology

Despite vastly reduced budgets, some companies continued to invest in technology, leading to breakthrough discoveries and prosperity. After years of research, DuPont's discovery of nylon, the first synthetic fiber, led to innovations in clothing and hundreds of applications ranging from parachutes to tires. The Plastic Age exploded as entrepreneurs found a variety of commercial applications for fiberglass. Commercial airlines spread their wings, making air travel more affordable to the traveling public. Discoveries in construction methods triggered a competition for the tallest skyscrapers. During the Depression, technology continued to advance, allowing entire new industries to flourish.

Redefining Worker Relationships

Unemployment steadily grew worse in the United States through the three initial depression years, reaching 25% at its peak. Rising labor tensions redefined the relationship between employees and employers. In some cases, labor unrest and unemployment pressures exploded into violent clashes. The cost and negative publicity of worker strikes ultimately forced management into painful settlements with organized labor and the formation of powerful unions.

Seeing the dire consequences of unrest and moved by an inner sense of loyalty for their workers, some employers refused to lay off workers, resorting instead to flexible work agreements. Notable cases include Armco Steel Company, Johnson & Johnson, and Eli Lilly.[37] Leaders at these companies engaged their employees in cost-saving activities, resulting in sustainable operational efficiency and voluntary payroll reductions. Those who kept their jobs saw their income drop by as much as one third. Some opted to reduce working hours.[38] In the end, this approach paid off as their committed workforce became a competitive advantage during the recovery.

Engaging Entrepreneurial Drive

In some cases, businesses and individuals had to reinvent themselves in order to forge a new future. Margaret F. Rudkin, the wife of a once-successful New York City stockbroker, faced a twist of fortune as their idyllic life unraveled. The Rudkins were accustomed to a life of affluence in high society, but after the stock market crash and her husband's polo accident, Mrs. Rudkin was forced to sell most of their assets. Rudkin emerged from the crisis as a dynamic and resourceful female entrepreneur. After a few failed startups, Rudkin turned an almost forgotten childhood hobby and her money-losing, 125-acre estate into her road to recovery.

Her talent for baking high quality bread became the basis for the successful Pepperidge Farms. "I never saw a cookbook in my house, and I never saw my grandmother or my mother write anything down. So my recipes came out of my head—just memories of how things tasted and looked."[39] She connected with her expanding clientele by personally vouching in the company's advertising for the natural ingredients and consistent quality of her products. Within a few years, her local enterprise was selling over 25,000 loaves of bread per week and expanding into related products. Like Margaret Rudkin, other individuals and businesses reinvented themselves and engaged their entrepreneurial drive to come out of difficult times successfully.

Restoring Trust

In an environment where many businesses were blighted by scandals, trust was nowhere more desperately needed than in the financial services industry. The image of the investment banker went from a man with a halo to one with horns and spiked tail.[40] It is in this caustic environment that Harold Stanley, one of the youngest partners at the prestigious J.P. Morgan & Company, decided, at age 42, to start over. With a handful of executives, Stanley formed Morgan, Stanley & Company. Using his connections in financial circles, Stanley issued over $1 billion in public offerings and placements in his first year.[41]

At a time when distrust and lack of integrity ran highest, Stanley represented unflinching ethics and uncompromising values. He based each transaction on a personal philosophy that business relationships, just like all human relationships, should be built on integrity, mutual respect, and balance.[42] Stanley adopted long-term relationships with customers, despite competitive and regulatory practices, in order to restore trust with his clients. Morgan, Stanley & Company emerged from the 1930s as one of the strongest and most reputable financial houses.

Strengthening Core Operations

Typical of the companies that came out of the Depression stronger is a relentless drive to excel at what they do best. The Pennsylvania Railroad Company is a good example of how a large and well-established employer expanded their services through innovative efficiency during the Depression. The investment was handsomely rewarded as the railroad was ready to tackle the increased transportation demands of World War II.

In 1935, Martin W. Clement headed the world's largest railway network. The Pennsylvania Railroad operated thousands of miles of track, employing about 130,000 employees and managing revenues of $350 million. Instead of scaling back when faced with a decline in business, the Pennsylvania Railroad decided to undertake a vast expansion and renovation.

Clement sought to improve the company's main assets by taking advantage of easily available labor, supplies, and government financing. He invested in lightweight electric locomotives and passenger cars that streamlined operating costs and reduced travel time to major U.S. cities. The company enhanced operational safety, drastically reducing the amount of worker injuries. Rail cars were also refurbished, providing the largest fleet of air-conditioned and comfortable passenger cars, thus attracting more long-distance travelers. Clement expanded the Pennsylvania Railroad services into a full transportation network able to deliver freight door-to-door from over 1,000 train stations. Making skillful use of government stimulus programs, like employing Public Works Administration workers, the railroad's revenues and operating income rose by 26% during the Depression years. The company became a symbol of operational efficiency.

The overarching attitude for success during tough times is best captured by the rise of the Rockefeller Center during the downturn. After receiving news of the market crash, John D. Rockefeller made one of the biggest bets in history. He had started a monumental real estate development project in the heart of Manhattan. "It was clear that there were only two courses open to me. One was to abandon the entire development. The other was to go forward with it in the definite knowledge that I myself would have to build it and finance it alone." There was a growing surplus of vacant real estate in the city, and Rockefeller had no foreseeable tenants for the building.

He decided to push ahead as the sole financial backer of the biggest office building project in history. The colossal edifice gave thousands of people jobs and hope through the grim times. Every effort was made to bestow the highest quality of design, construction, and décor to the building. The innovative structure attracted the headquarters of an emerging technology— the radio. Thus, 30 Rock became the broadcasting heart of the American mass media industry. The Rockefeller Center stands as a symbol of faith in the future, pointing to what winning organizations can do today to prosper.

Bet on the future.

~ Plaque at the Rockefeller Center

Learning from the Past

History repeats itself. What happened during the 1930s is curiously similar to what is happening now. We can draw obvious parallels from the past to learn from experience, gain perspective, and solve our current challenges.

History of the Dow

Dow Jones Industrial Average (DJI) from Oct. 1928 to Feb. 2009

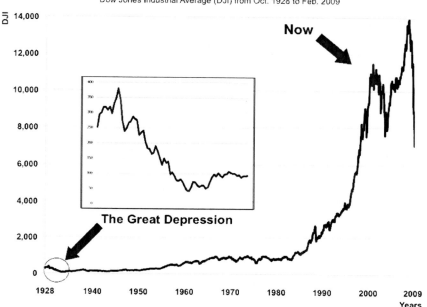

To put the scope of the current situation in perspective, we can compare the market variation to the Great Depression. The scale of the current economic crisis is far greater than the Depression. The size of the market now is about 35 times larger. The wide economic fluctuations that triggered the Great Depression look like a tiny blip compared with the drastic swings in the current financial markets.

In many respects, the current situation is without precedent. Besides the magnitude of the market, global reach is far greater. Because financial systems are far more integrated than they were in 1930, the current crisis became an instant global concern. Technology plays an accelerating role, increasing the speed and interaction of events. More than before, companies operate in a borderless world. People around the world are instantly and mutually affected. Governments, leaders, and workers respond much quicker to shifting conditions.

However, in many important ways, there are striking similarities between these time periods. The sequence of events after the crash of 1929 mimics recent events and decisions. Major financial institutions failed suddenly. Public sentiment turned from exuberance to anxiety. The government intervened with increased regulation and spending (though much faster and on a much greater scale now). Unemployment is rising like it did during the 1930s. People at all levels of society struggle to adjust to the shock, both financially and emotionally.

While we cannot predict our economic future, we can say that we are definitely not on the steady, upward Path of Ascent. The current conditions more closely correspond with the Roller Coaster Ride of unsuccessful change. Whether we continue on this path is yet to be seen.

What individuals and organizations can do to emerge from the crisis successfully is to learn from the principles that helped people and businesses succeed during the Great Depression. They should increase efficiency in a way that makes them stronger. Mindless budget cuts and recurring layoffs will ultimately hinder the organization's long-term capacity and the communities those organizations serve. A wiser approach is to engage everyone in the organization in sustainable cost savings.

The most valuable form of saving is adopting a thrifty culture. When efficiency becomes part of the organization's mindset, savings are sustainable. Otherwise, costs creep back up in other ways such as delayed expenses, contract fees, and special projects. In order to become an efficient organization, the leaders need to embrace frugality in their example.

**We develop an inspiring
view of life by focusing
on what we can learn
from the situation.**

In conjunction with efficiency, companies need to strategically invest in the future. The most successful companies will find ways to save costs by innovating. Just like the examples above, successful companies will become efficiency innovators by investing in technology, redefining worker relationships, engaging entrepreneurial drive, restoring trust with stakeholders, and strengthening core operations.

Similarly, as individuals and families, we need to become more frugal. We need to learn to differentiate between sustaining life or a lifestyle. Living within our means and being thrifty are essential skills for the years ahead. In the meantime, we can increase self-reliance by continuing to invest in the future of our family members. Advanced education, practical skills, healthy habits, and wholesome recreation are sound personal investments that should continue.

Leading change in the worst of times takes great courage. It would be much easier, given the prevailing gloom, to become discouraged. But challenging times provide the greatest opportunities for making a difference, often helping leaders find defining moments. While we may not fully understand why we have to go through a tough experience, we can develop an inspiring view of life by focusing on what we can learn from the situation.

We are not destined to repeat history if we can learn from it. The principles and practices on the Path of Ascent show how people and organizations can overcome the current crisis and come out stronger. Putting these principles to work will enhance our individual and collective condition. The future is determined only by our present actions.

Kites rise highest against the wind, not with it.

~Winston Churchill

Joining in the Ascent

Japan was devastated after World War II. All the large cities but Kyoto were severely damaged. Industries were forced to shut down and layoff their workers. Transportation networks were ruined, causing severe food shortages. Some of Japan's islands were occupied by the Soviet Union, and others were controlled by the United States. Over 500 military officers committed suicide right after the surrender and many hundreds more were executed. Japan was forbidden to ever lead a war again or to maintain an army. Little hope was left for the valiant country that believed itself fated to rule the world.

Among the reconstruction efforts, the United States sent production experts to teach the Japanese how to rebuild their fledgling economy. Relying on statistical control methods then familiar to the War Department, Japanese workers learned continuous improvement, a concept that resonated with the Buddhist philosophy *kaizen*.[43] Translated into English, *kaizen* means "change for the better," or simply "good change." The concept is rooted in the ancient teachings of Buddha.

Like the ascent principles, kaizen defines a process for making steady progress. The outcomes are to benefit the entire society, not just one particular individual at another's expense. This type of change has a significant and lasting impact on everyone involved. Kaizen delivers initial gains quickly and yields sustainable results over time.

In a few decades, Japan rebuilt its industry and rose from poverty to become one of the strongest economies in the world. This growth resulted in a quick rise in Japanese living standards, a more democratic society, and increased political stability. The kaizen approach has been associated with the impressive quality of Japanese manufacturing. It is widely used today for improving production quality and increasing efficiency in companies all over the world. The ascent principles and practices apply an equivalent process to human improvement.

The rise of Japan inspired other Asian countries on their own Path of Ascent. Hong Kong, South Korea, Singapore, and Taiwan, often referred to as the Asian Tigers, sustained fast growth rates, rapid industrialization, and higher standards of living between the 1960s and 1990s. These regions are still among the world's fastest growing economies, with highly skilled workforces specialized in areas where each country has a competitive advantage.

Establishing harmonious labor-management relations contributed to making this success possible.[44] These four regions focused on education, frugality, and export production to turn an impoverished people into a prosperous society. Embodying the concept is the formation of *kyochokai*, a type of industrial organization based on principles of cooperation and harmony that echo the ascent principles.

Growing up in Argentina I witnessed my native country's Path of Ascent during its trying return to democracy. Seven years of military dictatorship caused a gradual erosion of freedom that resulted in abuses of power and human rights violations. Average citizens had to valiantly defy a government that no longer represented them. The military junta finally lost power with the defeat in the Falklands War. On December 1983, Raúl Alfonsín was elected president of Argentina.

Securing the freedoms of a democratic government, however, required greater commitment from the people. Alfonsín's government struggled to strike a balance between bringing former oppressors to justice and gaining the support of belligerent armed forces. Public sentiment was volatile and required a great deal of discipline to rely on a democratic process.

Mounting tensions came to a head during the Easter week of 1987. During the President's Easter holiday retreat, a military faction marched to the federal government's plaza to exert their authority. On their march they were met by a military group loyal to the president, which started guerilla warfare in the streets of downtown Buenos Aires. The startling news shocked the nation at the time of religious celebration.

The media broadcasted live the rapid escalation of events that threatened civil war. The president flew into the scene by helicopter and addressed the nation from the balcony of the presidential house. He called on the Argentine people to vote in person for their democracy. Within minutes, over 50,000 citizens gathered peacefully around the government plaza in Buenos Aires. Many more gathered in government plazas at the main cities across the country, while millions more joined them through their televisions and radios.

As the advancing troops threatening the country's freedom made their way toward the presidential house, the people in the streets formed a human shield and started singing the national anthem. The scene of parents and children gathered against an oncoming line of tanks and armed forces evoked a great emotional response. The president himself advanced unarmed toward the leader of the rebels and asked for their surrender.

The leader of the mutiny requested amnesty for military personnel who committed crimes during the dictatorship. Argentina's future as a country came to a decision point. The choice was to go forward united, looking to the future, not to the past. As a nation, we had many wounds yet to heal and were faced with many challenges, but democracy was finally regained when the Argentine people stood united behind a greater cause. The president brought closure to the conflict and, speaking to the nation from his balcony, announced, "Happy Easter! The house is in order."

That was my last weekend in Argentina before immigrating to the United States. Departing my homeland with such memories gave me faith in the capacity of people everywhere to rise to a higher level. No matter how great our differences may be, more binds us together. The ascent principles and practices present a process to advance society.

Nowhere is the need for improvement greater than in helping the world's poor. In October 1998, Hurricane Mitch hit El Salvador, killing roughly 374 people and leaving approximately 55,900 people homeless. Heavy rainfall, flooding, and mudslides severely damaged the country's road network, making recovery slow. Two years later, while reconstruction was still underway, the country experienced a series of devastating earthquakes that destroyed or badly damaged nearly 25% of all private homes in the country and left 1.5 million people without housing. Sanitation and water systems in many communities were out of service. El Salvador, already one of the world's poorest countries, was stretched to the extreme.

The disasters prompted a tremendous response from the international community, governments, nongovernmental organizations, and private citizens alike. Following the earthquakes, I was invited to participate in a group of management consultants to aid in the reconstruction effort. We were to train a group of volunteers and local workers in their diverse humanitarian activities. Witnessing the condition of the locals struggling to put their lives together after the devastation touched me deeply. I was even more touched by the worldwide humanitarian efforts launched to assist them.

One afternoon, our group arrived after much difficulty at a remote village that had been left nearly inaccessible after the quakes. As our van stopped at the village center, about 100 people quickly lined up expecting some form of relief—food, medicine, supplies, anything! Their worn faces waited in anxious anticipation.

"Who wants to work?" announced Nora from the front of the line. Nora was the Salvadorean representative of a humanitarian service organization who guided us to the village. The crowd stood silent, their eyes fixed on us with great expectations. Nora repeated her question. "Who wants to work?" Again, silence. After Nora's third call, a woman broke out of the line and abruptly stated that there was no work for them to do; there were no jobs, no money, and no supplies. Nora reassured this woman, saying: "If you had an opportunity, do you want to work?" The woman replied in the affirmative. In a few more minutes about 30 people, mostly women, stood apart from the rest of the group in a line of those who wanted to work. Nora wished the rest of the bystanders a good day and politely told them that we had nothing more to offer them at the time. The gathered crowd slowly dispersed, sorely discouraged.

Turning to the group willing to work, Nora and the rest of us facilitated 30 startups through microfinance. In about three hours, we organized a community bank, issued $10 loans to each person and coached them individually on a business plan they could start right away to generate income for their families. Besides receiving access to a modest amount of capital, this group of destitute people turned into 30 entrepreneurs with a vision for the future and a plan to carry it out.

Day after day our group traveled the rain forest roads of El Salvador providing hands-on training to similar groups at different stages of development. At each community bank, members awaited the meetings, eager to make their loan repayment and learn more skills. Their commitment to pay the loan back at the rate of $1 a week reflected a strong sense of integrity and self-respect. Most startups relied on existing talents for making food, making clothes, or raising chickens. We helped them think through a business plan. Our awe at this simple process for increasing self-reliance grew as the days went on. But Nora kept saying, "Wait until you meet Maria, the president of our most outstanding community bank!"

Toward the end of our trip, we finally met Maria. Approaching her place, we noticed an unusual number of people traveling on foot or by donkey alongside the road. Some were carrying construction materials on top of their heads or on their animals. As we reached our destination, we saw a large gathering of travelers lining up in front of a cinderblock three-room house—a large local dwelling! They were making banking transactions in front of Maria's house, borrowing, making payments, and acquiring basic materials. A bank clerk sat on a stool, keeping records of each transaction in a notebook.

Nora proudly introduced us to Maria, the local community bank president. She was a very short woman of marked native features and graying hair. She shook our hands and with great joy showed us her modest home, which to her was nothing short of a miracle. Then she took us to her backyard. Engulfed by the jungle, she had cleared a small area where she had created a vegetable garden, using automobile tires and micro-gardening techniques. She proceeded to show us a 100-chicken coop built on the side of the house, which had started with only 5 chickens. Back on her porch, Maria brought to us her greatest joy: portraits of each of her three daughters taken at their college graduations. One was now a lawyer, another a doctor of medicine, and the third a professor at a university in Chicago. Maria's face beamed as she told us how she had been able to go to Chicago once to attend a microfinance conference, with all expenses paid by her daughter.

We shared in her happiness. Sensing our delight, she said to us, "Let me show you were I lived before you came." She took us down a path a short distance from her house to a badly torn animal shelter the size of a dog house. The dirt floor was covered with straw and feathers. Not one of us could imagine a human being living there. She kept pointing to it while laughing and crying at the same time, saying: "I lived like an animal!" We could not hold back from crying and laughing with her as we realized the change in Maria's life, her three daughters, and the hundreds of people in the neighboring community.

Microfinance provides financial services to the poor, but done correctly it provides much more. The process brings vision to the hopeless, skills to the unlearned, and opportunity to the destitute. The fundamental principles and practices we taught the people of El Salvador represent, in their simplest form, the Path of Ascent.

Living organisms respond to crisis through adaptation and decisive growth. An aspen grove, for example, migrates, diversifies, centralizes, and mutates depending on the external environment. The complex network of roots that links aspen trees ferries nutrients from one part of the grove to another, constantly transferring vital resources where they are most needed. During years of drought, the entire aspen forest concentrates around lakes and their run offs. As droughts end, aspen rapidly spread shoots into diverse terrain. Within a few years, the new growth easily dwarfs the previous size of the forest. As beautifully described in a poem by Douglas Malloch, wind, snow, and strife bring out the best in nature.

> *The tree that never had to fight*
> *for sun and sky and air and light,*
> *but stood out in the open plain*
> *and always got its share of rain,*
> *never became a forest king*
> *but lived and died a scrubby thing.*
>
> *Good timber does not grow with ease,*
> *the stronger the wind, the stronger the trees,*
> *the further the sky, the greater the length,*
> *the more the storm, the more the strength.*
> *By sun and cold, by rain and snow,*
> *In trees and men good timbers grow.*
>
> ~Good Timber, by Douglas Malloch

Over 20 years ago, my life changed significantly as I arrived in America. With little else but a dream for a better future, I had left behind the security of home and family. My first years as a young immigrant were often difficult and lonely. Faced with a new language and culture, I decided to learn all I could.

Writing a single-page essay in English was an arduous task, often consuming several days and multiple revisions. Despite the obvious disadvantage, I decided to master the language and study English literature. I never imagined that one day I would write an entire book in what once was a foreign tongue. The process of diligent study and numerous revisions gave me not only a new language, but also the discipline for personal growth.

The Path of Ascent is real and evident in every aspect of life. The concept is based on the simple premise that applying the correct principles for growth invariably leads people and organizations to a higher level. The same has been proven to be true in my personal life, in my work with client organizations, and at the Change Masters. It worked for successful companies during good economic times and times of downturn. Looking around, we can see that every change in society that elevates the human condition is based on individual choices to live such principles.

The settings may vary, but the underlying principles are the same. When faced with a challenge, we have to choose between two paths. The easy way out is to change others to get what we want. This approach seeks quick-fix solutions that never fully satisfy and end up causing more trouble. Unfortunately, this is the most popular road. The higher road requires that we change from the inside out, reaching out higher, and making it possible for everyone to live a better life. The upward course is clearly the best option. The choice is ours to ascend.

The time is always right
to do what is right.

~Martin Luther King Jr.

Research Appendix

The ideas presented in this book result, for the most part, from my day-to-day consulting work with leaders, teams, and organizations. Consequently, I present the concepts as a summary of personal experiences, organized in a way to help business leaders, mid-level managers, and front-line supervisors achieve better results.

The Five Ascent Principles provide a comprehensive framework for mastering personal and organizational change. The complete model includes five sequential steps, based on corresponding principles and practices. When applying each of the Ascent Principles, one can expect a predictable positive outcome, while reducing the negative influence of a widening gap. The model outlines a course of action for any person, team, or organization desiring to improve. A visual representation of that course is provided by the Path of Ascent, showing a steady upward trend. This trend is not only symbolic of sustainable improvement, but it reflects the actual stock price performance of well-known companies that changed successfully in the last 15 years. The chart on the following page describes the model.

Implied in this model is the premise that applying the Five Ascent Principles™ lead to successful personal and organizational change. On the other hand, failed change is the predictable outcome of neglecting these principles partially or entirely. I present the model as a hypothesis—a proposition of how things work. Then, I proceed to validate this model with data collected from the study of 50 companies, comparing the 10

The Five Ascent Principles

Gaps	Process	Principle	Practices	Outcomes
Low Trust	1. Envision	Create the story of success	• Find common purpose • Create the story of success • Describe the envisioned future • Promote the story of success	**Purpose**
Lack of Focus	2. Evaluate	Seize the opportunity for change	• Define strategic objectives • Listen to stakeholder feedback • Clarify the strategic plan • Communicate the strategic plan	**Direction**
Poor Capability	3. Empower	Develop capacity from strengths	• Deploy change champions • Develop core competencies • Assess risk and resistance • Define a more effective process	**Capacity**
Weak Commitment	4. Engage	Inspire collaboration and teamwork	• Identify engagement drivers • Create the engagement conditions • Engage others by example • Coach for high performance	**Commitment**
Delayed Results	5. Evolve	Achieve increasingly better results	• Identify desired results • Set specific goals with milestones • Report progress on key indicators • Conduct business reviews	**Results**

most successful (Change Masters) and the 10 most unsuccessful (Change Failures) transformations.

This appendix describes the research criteria behind the selection of successful and unsuccessful companies during a time of change. Defining the success of a change initiative is subject to how one balances different variables and observations. An element of judgment has been used in selecting the finalists that make up the Change Masters and Change Failures.

The original list of companies studied was compiled from publicly traded companies from which there are financial data and news articles available. The list identifies companies that underwent a significant transformation—not just an incremental improvement. The research focuses on changes occurring in the last 15 years to ensure that the changes occurred during a similar economic business environment.

The actual period of the change for each organization is defined by a start and an end date, typically three to four years apart. The start date is indicated by a recognizable event, such as the launch of a new strategy, or the appointment of a new senior executive. The end date represents a natural end of the transformation period, usually indicated by the departure of key members of the management team, a shift in direction, or a new set of priorities.

The following chart shows the initial list of companies analyzed, their stock symbol, and the change period studied.

Companies Analyzed			
#	Company	Symbol	Period
1	3 Com	COMS	2001–2005
2	3M	MMM	2000–2004
3	Abbott Laboratories	ABT	1999–2003
4	Agere Systems	AGR	2002–2006
5	Apple	AAPL	2001–2005
6	Archer Daniels Midland	ADM	1999–2003
7	Avaya	AV	2001–2005

8	Barclays	BCS	1999–2003
9	Bay Networks	BAY	1995–1997
10	Best Buy	BBY	2002–2006
11	Boeing	BA	1996–2000
12	Brocade Communications Systems	BRCD	1999–2003
13	Brunswick	BC	2000–2004
14	Caterpillar	CAT	2003–2006
15	DaimlerChrysler	DCX	2000–2004
16	Dell	DELL	1999–2001
17	Delta Airlines	DALRQ	1999–2003
18	Eastman Kodak	EK	2000–2004
19	Electronic Data Systems	EDS	2003–2006
20	Ford	F	1999–2003
21	General Electric	GE	1995–1999
22	General Electric	GE	2001–2005
23	General Motors	GM	2000–2004
24	Hewlett-Packard	HPQ	1999–2003
25	Hilton Hotels	HLT	1997–2002
26	IBM	IBM	1995–1999
27	Ingram Micro	IM	2000–2004
28	Intel	INTC	1994–1999
29	Lucent	LU	2000–2004
30	McDonald's	MCD	2003–2006
31	Motorola	MOT	2004–2006
32	New York Times	NYT	2002–2006
33	Nissan	NSANY	2000–2004
34	Nokia	NOK	1999–2003
35	Nordstrom	JWN	2000–2004
36	Nortel Networks	NT	1998–2002
37	Procter & Gamble	PG	2000–2004
38	Qwest Communications	Q	2002–2006

39	RadioShack	RSH	2000–2004
40	Redback Networks	RBAK	2001–2005
41	Schering-Plough	SGP	2003–2006
42	Sony	SNE	1999–2003
43	Symbol Technologies	SBL	2003–2006
44	Telefónica de España	TEF	2000–2004
45	The Home Depot	HD	2000–2004
46	Time Warner	TWX	2000–2004
47	Tyco International	TYC	2002–2006
48	VeriSign	VRSN	2003–2006
49	Whirlpool	WHR	1999–2003
50	Xerox	XRX	2001–2005

The criteria for determining the degree of success of the change initiative takes into account five key conditions:

- **Intentional:** The company publicly announced a significant change through organic growth, acquisitions, global expansion, operational improvements, or innovative products.
- **Goals Met:** The goals of the change were clearly met or exceeded, as reported by business journals and trade articles.
- **Significant:** The company financials indicate a significant improvement during the change period.
- **Legitimate:** The change was seen as a legitimate achievement, without relying on external market conditions, economic trends, or artificial accounting practices.
- **Sustainable:** The change was sustainable, meaning that the achievements were considered an actual improvement, likely to remain (unless adversely affected by changes in external market conditions).

Ranking the original list of 50 companies using the above stated criteria identifies two sets of companies—the Change Masters and the Change Failures. Each group shows a different approach to leading change. Comparing both groups through news articles, publications, and interviews of employees who worked at these companies reveals the strong or clear influence

#	Company	Envision Purpose	Evaluate Direction	Empower Capacity	Engage Commitment	Evolve Results
Ascent Principles at the Change Masters						
1	Intel	●	●	●	◓	●
2	Apple	●	●	◓	◓	◓
3	General Electric	◓	●	◓	●	◓
4	IBM	◒	●	◓	◓	●
5	Caterpillar	◒	●	◓	◒	◓
6	McDonald's	◒	◓	◒	◒	◓
7	VeriSign	●	●	●	◓	●
8	Nissan	◓	●	●	●	●
9	3M	◒	●	●	●	●
10	Xerox	●	◒	●	●	◒
Ascent Principles at the Change Failures						
1	Nortel Networks	○	◒	○	○	○
2	3 Com	○	○	◒	○	◒
3	Dell	○	●	◒	○	◒
4	Ford	◒	○	◒	○	◒
5	Eastman Kodak	◒	◒	◒	◒	◒
6	New York Times	◒	◒	○	◒	◒
7	General Motors	○	◒	◒	○	◒
8	RadioShack	◒	●	◒	◓	◒
9	Qwest Communications	○	○	◒	◒	◒
10	Hewlett-Packard	◒	◒	◒	◒	◒

● Strong Influence ◓ Clear Influence ◒ Minor Influence ○ Little or No Influence

of the Five Ascent Principles at the Change Masters. On the other hand, there is a tendency toward minor or little influence of such principles at the Change Failures.

In addition to this research, further evidence comes from professional experiences as a first-hand witness of successful and unsuccessful change at client organizations. The stories I share in this book represent actual cases. In order to maintain confidentiality, where appropriate, the names and other minor particulars have been altered, without distorting the essential reality of the experience.

In the accounts I present, there may be some simplification in order to abbreviate the presentation. I focus by choice on the highlights of each case to present the reader with a concise point. It is important to note, however, that through the periods of confusion and frustration inherent in any change process, the key concepts were in every aspect actual and material components of the outcome. The Ascent Principles played an important role behind the success stories at each of my clients. Their cases reinforce the relevance of the Ascent model.

This book makes frequent references to personal change as the source of larger changes in teams and organizations. I firmly believe that the two are inseparably connected. One source of change is constantly influencing the other. Sustainable progress initiates from the inside-out, from individuals who improve themselves and then influence their environment for the better.

The primary contribution of the Path of Ascent is to identify the process, principles, and practices leading to a successful change. Understanding the essential difference between improving and merely changing, we are able to predict the likely outcomes of an initiative. Moreover, we are able to Ascend at work and in our lives.

Notes

1.   Andy Reinhardt, "Bay Networks' Mr. House Finds His Fixer-Upper," *BusinessWeek* (Feb. 2, 1998).

2.   Anne P. Massey, Mitzi M. Montoya-Weiss, and Tony M. O'Driscoll, "Knowledge Management in Pursuit of Performance: Insights from Nortel Networks," *MIS Quarterly* 26/3 (Sept. 2002), 269–289.

3.   Bill Roberts, "Top 50 Electronics Mergers and Acquisitions." *Electronic Business* (Jan. 1, 1999).

4.   Ibid., 14.

5.   Gary Gereffi and Vivek Wadhwa, *Framing the Engineering Outsourcing Debate: Placing the United States on a Level Playing Field with China and India* (Duke University, 2005).

6.   Organisation of Economic Co-operation and Development (OECD), quoted in *Measuring Up: National Report Card on American Education* (measuringup.highereducation.org).

7.   Anthony Carnevale and Donna Desrochers, *Standards for What?* (Princeton, N.J.: Educational Testing Service, 2003), 69.

8.   *SHRM Research, 2006 Access to Human Capital.*

9.   IBM Global CEO Study.

10.   U.S. Bureau of Labor Statistics, workforce survey between 1979–1994.

11.   Pierre Mourier and Martin R. Smith, *Conquering Organizational Change: How to Succeed Where Most Companies Fail* (Atlanta, GA: CEP Press, 2001).

12.   Tom James, "Quick! Fix the Hippo: Leadership Instincts and Organizational Ecosystems," (unpublished manuscript).

13.   Mark Arzoumanian, "Making The Grade: Norampac's Board Mill in Burnaby, British Columbia Surmounted Serious Financial and Production Problems As It Refocused Its Market" (http://findarticles.com/p/articles/mi_m3116/is_12_86/ai_n27573469).

14.   Ibid.

15.   Heinrich Harrer, *The White Spider: The Classic Account of the Ascent of the Eiger* (Penguin Putman, 1998).

16.   Jeffrey L. Cruikshank, *The Apple Way* (New York: McGraw-Hill, 2006), 13.

17.   M. Moritz, *The Little Kingdom: The Private Story of Apple Computer* (New York: William Morrow, 1984), 14.

18.   "History of Computer Design" (www.landsnail.com/apple/local/design/design.html).

19.   "Apple Cuts 1,300 Jobs, Shifts Focus; Firm Reports Loss, New Emphasis On Top-Of-Line Macs," *Seattle Post-Intelligencer.*

20.   AAPL, Google Finance, split adjusted.

21.   "2008 American Customer Satisfaction Index" (http://www.theacsi.org).

22.   Clay Chandler, "Nissan Maps Plan To Remodel Itself," *The Washington Post.*

23.   Andrew Haeg, "A Leaner 3M," Minnesota Public Radio, April 22, 2002 (http://news.minnesota.publicradio.org/features/200204/22_haega_3mupdate/).

24.   Andrew Haeg, "McNerney's Challenge in the 'Culture of Innovation,'" Minnesota Public Radio, Dec. 5, 2000.

25.   Vikki Valentine, "Health for the Masses: China's 'Barefoot Doctors'" (http://www.npr.org/templates/story/story.php?storyId=4990242).

26.   Bill George and Andrew N. McLean, "Anne Mulcahy: Leading Xerox through the Perfect Storm" Harvard Business School (Case Study 9-405-050, Jan. 26, 2005).

27.   Betsy Morris, "The Accidental CEO," *Fortune* (June 23, 2003), 58.

28.   Bill George, "America's Best Leaders: Anne Mulcahy, Xerox CEO," *US News and World Report* (Nov. 19, 2008).

29.   "The Global Workforce Study" (Towers-Perrin, 2007).

30.   Peter Flade, "Employee Engagement Drives Shareholder Value," (Feb. 13, 2008).

31.   Mike Desmarais, "Contact Center Employee Satisfaction & Customer Satisfaction Link" (SQM Group for Manpower, 2005).

32.   John Engen, "Are Your Employees Truly Engaged?" (March 2008).

33.   Robert J. Vance, "Employee Engagement and Commitment," (SHRM Foundation, 2006).

34.   Story inspired by Dale Carnegie, *How to Win Friends and Influence People* (New York: Pocket Books, 1982), 42.

35.   Excerpts from "A Conversation with Gordon Moore: Moore's Law" (ftp://download.intel.com/museum/Moores_Law/Video-Transcripts/Excepts_A_Conversation_with_Gordon_Moore.pdf).

36.   Jeffrey E. Garten, "Andy Grove Made The Elephant Dance: Intel's Boss, Who Retires Soon, Kept the Giant Perennially Nimble," *Businessweek* (http://www.businessweek.com/magazine/content/05_15/b3928036_mz007.htm).

37.   B. C. Forbes, *America's Fifty Foremost Business Leaders* (New York: Forbes, 1948), 215–20.

38.   David M. Kennedy, *Freedom from Fear* (New York: Oxford University Press, 1999), 163. Michael E. Parrish, *Anxious Decades: America in Prosperity and Depression, 1929–1941* (New York: Norton, 1992).

39. Margaret Rudkin, *The Margaret Rudkin Pepperidge Farm Cookbook* (New York: Margaret Rudkin, 1963), 14.

40. Vincent P. Carosso, *Investment Banking in America: A History* (Cambridge, MA: Harvard University Press, 1970), 300.

41. Morgan Stanley & Company, "A Summary of Financing 1935–1965" (internal publication).

42. Harold Stanley, *Competitive Bidding for New Issues of Corporate Securities* (New York: Morgan Stanley & Co., 1939), 2.

43. Jim Huntzinger, "The Roots of Lean: Training within Industry—the Origin of Kaizen," *AME Target* 18/1: 13.

44. cf. W. Dean Kinzley, *Industrial Harmony in Modern Japan: The Invention of a Tradition* (London & New York: Routledge, 1991).

Index

About the Author

Juan Riboldi is the President and Principal Advisor at Ascent Advisor, a consulting firm specializing in leadership and organizational change. Juan is an accomplished consultant, executive coach, public speaker, and author.

With only a loan from friends and family and a vision for the future, Juan came to the United States from Argentina in search of opportunities. As an international student, Juan obtained academic degrees in Industrial Design, English Literature, Statistics, Business Management, and Organizational Behavior.

Over the last 20 years, Juan has consulted in various countries with leaders of corporations such as IBM, Sony Pictures, Cisco Systems, General Mills, Financial Times, Blue Care Network, Veteran's Health Administration, Farmers Insurance, the Department of Defense, Costco, and Nissan.

Juan has taught executive courses at Harvard Business School, Pepperdine University, and Brigham Young University. An avid amateur triathlete and sailor, Juan lives with his family at the foothills of the Wasatch mountains.

Ascent Advisor

Ascent Advisor is a management consulting firm. We are a trusted advisor to progressive leaders seeking for performance breakthroughs. We bring the capability for mastering change.

We have distilled years of experience into a proven process and tools for making change work. We don't offer pre-packaged solutions, nor do we insert ourselves to run your business. We do however, work besides our clients to achieve results in 100 days.

We engage senior leaders in defining change strategies, coach change champions in implementing improvement initiatives, and train all the employees in the principles of change. This approach ensures that benefits are realized and replicated.

SERVICES

Assessments: Link people with results

Workshops: Apply Change Principles

Certification: Build Change Capacity

100-day Projects: Achieve Critical Results

For additional information contact:

Ascent Advisor
www.ascent-advisor.com
info@ascent-advisor.com
Toll Free: 800-679-2881
Telephone: 801-375-1300

CPSIA information can be obtained at www.ICGtesting.com
Printed in the USA
BVOW012110290112

281518BV00003BA/1/P

9 780982 464700